WHO AND WHEN?

The
ROMANTICS

Artists, Writers,
and Composers

WHO AND WHEN?

The ROMANTICS

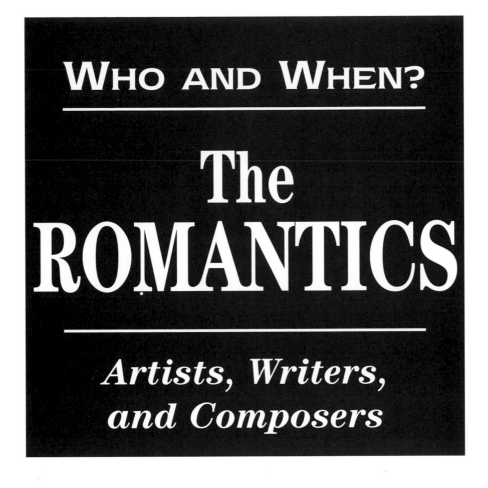

Artists, Writers, and Composers

Edited by Sarah Halliwell

RSVP
RAINTREE STECK-VAUGHN
P U B L I S H E R S
The Steck-Vaughn Company

Austin, Texas

Steck-Vaughn Company

First published 1998 by Raintree Steck-Vaughn Publishers,
an imprint of Steck-Vaughn Company.
Copyright © 1998 Marshall Cavendish Limited.

Library of Congress Cataloging-in-Publication Data
The Romantics: artists, writers, and composers / edited by Sarah Halliwell
p. cm. -- (Who and When?: v. 4)
Includes bibliographical references and index.
Summary: Introduces some of the major artists, writers, and composers that flourished
in Europe and the United States during the Romantic era in the late eighteenth
and early nineteenth centuries.
ISBN 0-8172-4729-7
1. Artists -- Europe -- Biography -- Juvenile literature. 2. Romanticism in art -- Europe --
Juvenile literature. [1. Artists. 2. Authors. 3. Composers. 4. Romanticism.]
I. Halliwell, Sarah. II. Series: Who and When?: v. 4.
NX542.R668 1998
700'.92'2--dc21
[B]

97-29096
CIP
AC

Printed and bound in Italy
1 2 3 4 5 6 7 8 9 0 LE 02 01 00 99 98 97

Marshall Cavendish Limited
Managing Editor: Ellen Dupont
Project Editor: Sarah Halliwell
Senior Editor: Andrew Brown
Senior Designer: Richard Newport
Designer: Richard Shiner
Picture administrator: Vimu Patel
Production: Craig Chubb
Index: Susan Bosanko

Raintree Steck-Vaughn
Publishing Director: Walter Kossmann
Project Manager: Joyce Spicer
Editor: Shirley Shalit

Consultants:
Anthea Peppin, National Gallery, London;
Dr. Andrew Hadfield, University of Wales;
Jonathan Kulp, University of Texas.

Contributors:
Iain Zaczek, Lorien Kite, Andrew Brown,
Sarah Halliwell.

CONTENTS

INTRODUCTION

Romanticism was a wide-ranging movement that dominated European culture in the first half of the 19th century. It affected writers, artists, and composers—in a variety of different ways. Originally, the word came from the medieval "romances"—stirring tales of adventure and love—but by the end of the 18th century, it had gained a quite different meaning. It was now used to describe the reaction against the neoclassical style of the previous age.

Neoclassicism had stood for control, order, reason, and strict artistic rules. The Romantics rejected all this. Instead, they admired the power of the imagination, the strength of wild emotions, and personal freedom. In particular, they supported individuals' struggles against authority, echoing the battle for democracy that was taking place throughout Europe. Inspired by the French Revolution of 1789, which had resulted in the downfall of a hated king, other nations waged war on their rulers. In the 1820s, the people of Russia revolted against the czar, and the citizens of Poland and Greece struggled to overthrow their foreign overlords.

The Romantics committed themselves wholeheartedly to such causes. In France, the artist Eugène Delacroix (*see page 28*) celebrated the July Revolution of 1830 with his painting *Liberty Leading the People*, while the music of Polish composer Frédéric Chopin (*see page 76*) was full of patriotic fervor for his enslaved homeland. The English poet Lord Byron (*see page 38*) went one stage further, traveling to Greece to help rebels in their fight for independence. Although some Romantics paid tribute to military leaders—German composer Ludwig van Beethoven (*see page 64*), for example, dedicated works to the French emperor Napoleon Bonaparte—they also focused on outcasts. Heathcliff, the brooding loner who suffers rejection in Emily Brontë's *Wuthering Heights* (*see page 58*), is in many ways the typical Romantic hero—passionate and intense. There was also a new sympathy for the common man. In earlier pictures of battles, artists had usually focused on glorious deeds and acts of bravery. But Romantic painters such as the Spaniard Francisco de Goya (*see page 8*) and Delacroix preferred to highlight the victims of warfare.

The shift in taste extended to other fields. In their retreat from reason, the Romantics chose subjects that were strange, mysterious, and exotic. Insanity was a popular theme. Goya produced powerful images of the insane, while Charlotte Brontë's novel

Jane Eyre (*see page 58*) revolved around a madwoman. Horror and the supernatural were also very much in fashion. Goya portrayed monsters and witches in some of his prints, while the climax of Hector Berlioz's *Symphonie Fantastique* (*see page 72*) featured disturbing, drug-induced hallucinations and witchcraft. In literature, Mary Shelley's *Frankenstein* (*see page 46*) and Edgar Allan Poe's short stories (*see page 54*) were pioneering works, copied by a host of imitators. These tales were described as "Gothic," since they captured the spirit of the Middle Ages, when the Gothic style flourished in painting and architecture. The Romantics took inspiration from this period—rather than from ancient Greece and Rome, as the previous generation had done—because they saw it as an age of mystery and enchantment. This mood is apparent in the atmospheric poems of John Keats (*see page 42*), the colorful characters of Victor Hugo's *Hunchback of Notre Dame* (*see page 50*), and the sinister ruins of Caspar David Friedrich's paintings (*see page 14*).

Along with their taste for distant times and bizarre subjects, the Romantics focused their imagination on nature. Here, dramatic changes in the countryside shaped their attitudes. The invention of the steam engine in 1765 had ushered in a new age, the Industrial Revolution. For centuries, most workers had toiled in the fields, growing and harvesting crops. But now, many of them spent their time in factories, the "dark satanic mills," as the English poet William Blake described them. Many longed for the countryside of old. In his poems, William Wordsworth (*see page 34*) celebrated the beauty of the Lake District in northern England, believing that God's presence could be felt in nature. A similar outlook featured in the paintings of J.M.W. Turner (*see page 18*) and Friedrich. In both cases, human figures appear small and in-significant, compared with the awesome power of the elements.

The Romantics' love of nature later spread to the United States. Inspired by Thomas Cole, the first great American landscape artist and founder of the Hudson River School, 19th-century painters such as Frederick Church and Albert Bierstadt pro-duced monumental works portraying the grandeur of the American countryside. Their views of Niagara Falls, the Rocky Mountains, and the West expressed the idea that God was present in America's natural phenomena, implying that He looked favorably on the country. This idea coincided with the belief in "Manifest Destiny," the view that America's westward expansion was fulfilling the will of God.

FRANCISCO DE GOYA

One of the most original artists of his age, Goya produced glittering portraits of his royal patrons—and also some of the darkest and most intense images in art. Both his technique and approach were bold and uncompromising.

Francisco Goya y Lucientes was born on March 30, 1746, in the village of Fuendetodos, western Spain. His father was a craftsman, and Francisco wanted to work in a similar field. It would, however, take him many years to develop his talent.

SLOW PROGRESS
At the age of 14, Goya was apprenticed to a provincial artist, José Luzán, but it was not long before he found a more distinguished teacher, Francisco Bayeu. Bayeu was an official painter at the court of the Spanish king. It seemed likely that working for him would help Goya's own career prospects, so in 1764, he traveled to Madrid to join Bayeu's studio. There, his progress was slow. He failed to gain entrance to the San Fernando Academy of Art, and his only success came during a trip to Italy in 1770, when he won a minor award.

On his return to Spain, Goya renewed his links with Bayeu. He married his teacher's sister, Josefa, in 1773. A year later, Bayeu found him a job at the Royal Tapestry Factory of Santa Barbara in Madrid. Here, Goya sketched out decorative scenes, which weavers then wove into tapestries. The task did not allow Goya much opportunity to use his imagination. Even so, this was to be his main job for the next 18 years.

In his spare time, Goya painted portraits and religious pictures. It was these that helped him to gradually build up his reputation. In 1780, he was made a member of the San Fernando Academy, and in 1789, he became royal painter at the court of the newly crowned king, Charles IV. Goya celebrated by adding "de" to his name, to make himself sound more aristocratic.

This was also a happy time in other ways. The extra money allowed him to indulge in his hobbies. He bought a two-wheeled carriage, which he drove

Self-portrait, c.1790, by Francisco de Goya
This unusual self-portrait, showing the artist at his easel, displays Goya's bold and vigorous painting technique.

around the streets of Madrid at a reckless speed. And in 1784, he and Josefa had a son, Javier—the only one of their children to survive into adulthood.

A DRAMATIC CHANGE

This blissful period did not last for long. In 1792, Goya suffered a severe illness, which paralyzed him for a time and left him deaf for the rest of his life. This setback changed his entire outlook on life. He was away from the court for about a year, and during this time he began to paint a series of small oil paintings of "fantasy and invention."

> "To perpetrate by means of the brush the most notable and heroic actions ... against the tyrant."
> (Goya's aim in painting the Spanish people's fight against French invaders in 1808)

This type of picture, which probed the darker side of the human imagination, occupied him more and more. Eventually, he worked the images into a series of prints entitled *Los Caprichos*.

It seems that Goya's illness made him restless about his career. He was highly successful; many people wanted him to paint pictures for them. Yet, on the other hand, he felt he had lost his free-

GOYA'S WORLD OF FANTASY

With his bizarre and nightmarish images, Goya prepared the way for the birth of Romanticism.

In his life, Goya produced hundreds of prints. While in some he took bullfighting or war as his subject, in others he used macabre images to attack the social customs and beliefs of his day.

In his first major print series, *Los Caprichos*—or *Fantasies*—of the late 1790s, Goya created one of his most famous pictures, *The Sleep of Reason Produces Monsters* (*right*). In this, a sleeping artist is surrounded by flying bat-like creatures. The print challenged the 18th-century idea that knowledge is reached only through Reason—cold, logical thought—without the use of instinct, intuition, or emotion.

dom, since he could not paint subjects of his own choice. "Work done to order gives no opportunity," he complained, "as it does not allow *capricho* [fantasy] and invention to have free play."

As a result, Goya left his job at the tapestry factory and tried to become a more independent artist. The *Caprichos*, with their lively images of witches and madmen, were a first step in this

Goya's vision expressed the belief that free, unrestrained imagination can open up a whole new world that Reason alone could never reveal. By dealing with the themes of nightmare, fantasy, and creative freedom, Goya was addressing the issues that would inspire the Romantic artists and writers over the coming decades.

daring direction. Goya did not give up his position at court, however, and, after he had recovered from his illness, these duties began to occupy him once again. In 1795, on the death of Bayeu, he was made director of painting at the San Fernando Academy and, four years later, he became the king's chief painter.

Goya owed this promotion to his supreme skill as a portraitist. He had an extraordinary skill for bringing his subjects to life on canvas. This was due partly to his clever analysis of their character—and partly to his own remarkable technique.

Unlike most other painters of the time, Goya applied his paint very freely, leaving out small details and sharp outlines. He explained: "Where does one see lines in nature? I see no lines or details. I don't count each hair on the head of a passer-by.... There is no reason why my brush should see more than I do." This made his portraits seem very natural, almost like a modern snapshot. In fact, though, he carefully planned and sketched out every turn of the head and every gesture in advance.

CAUGHT UP IN POLITICS

Goya produced more than 200 portraits during his lifetime, many of them showing his master, King Charles IV. Charles was a weak ruler with a feeble grasp of international politics, and his mistakes helped plunge his country into chaos. In 1808, the French army swept into Spain and placed Napoleon's brother, Joseph, on the throne. For the next five years, the Spanish people fought a bloody war of resistance against the French invaders.

Goya was appalled at the suffering caused by the war. In around 1810, he began work on a series of prints—*The Disasters of War*—that record the consequences of the fighting. His prints show horrific scenes of cruelty, greed, and starvation. Both sides inflict and suffer shocking atrocities, underlining Goya's belief that in war, no one wins.

The Third of May, 1808, (1814), by Francisco de Goya
On May 2, 1808, the Spanish people revolted against the French occupation of their country. The French took vicious reprisals the next day, murdering hundreds of Spaniards. Goya's painting depicts the ruthless brutality of the anonymous executioners and the terror of the victims. With bold and shocking honesty, the image shows the grim reality of war.

Goya had little choice other than to cooperate with the new regime. He agreed to swear loyalty to the new king and, in 1811, he accepted the Royal Order of Spain from him.

This honor was later to prove an embarrassment to Goya, when the Spanish expelled the French and Ferdinand VII, Charles IV's son, came to the throne. Goya offered the excuse that he had never worn the medal, and backed this up in 1814 by painting two impressive pictures as a present for the new king. These were *The Second of May, 1808,* and *The Third of May, 1808,* which commemorated his countrymen's brave fight against the French.

The period after the war was a gloomy time in Spain. The universities and theaters were closed, newspapers were censored, and the Inquisition—an ancient religious body with terrible powers—was brought back to control the morals of the Spanish people. Goya himself was summoned to appear before it. He was questioned about a painting of a naked woman, which was considered to be obscene.

Goya had other problems too. He was the target of vicious gossip: His wife Josefa had died in 1812, and he was now having an affair with a married woman, Leocadia Weiss. Such troubles probably help to explain the depressing mood of Goya's later paintings.

The attitude of the new king did nothing to improve the situation. Although Ferdinand continued to employ

---

"Light and shade play upon atrocious horrors."
(Charles Baudelaire on *The Third of May, 1808*)

Goya, he took very little interest in the artist's work. Realizing this, Goya left the court in 1815. Four years later, the artist suffered another serious illness, which almost killed him.

THE "BLACK PAINTINGS"
As before, this brush with death stirred the artist's imagination, prompting him to create the most astonishing pictures of his entire career. These were the famous "Black Paintings," which Goya produced between 1820 and 1823 on the walls of his new house—known as the "House of the Deaf Man."

Goya painted 14 murals in all, using a somber range of blacks, grays, and browns. Filled with pessimism, he let his imagination dwell on the themes of old age, suffering, and death. Although

the exact meaning of these "Black" pictures is unclear, the dark mood and atmosphere is very powerful.

The paintings are extraordinary, not only for their bizarre and often nightmarish subjects, but also for Goya's free and spontaneous technique. Painting in this way, Goya was far ahead of his time. He painted the pictures purely for his own interest, and never expected the public to see them—a startling idea in the early 19th century. At the time, most artists painted to fulfill commissions and make a living, rather than to please themselves.

Soon after he had completed the "Black Paintings," Goya left Spain and moved to Bordeaux in France, where he lived with Leocadia. Friends thought that he now looked "old, slow, and feeble," but his mind was alert, and his passion for art was as strong as ever. He finally died of a stroke on April 16, 1828, at the age of 82, and was buried in France. His remains were eventually returned to Spain in 1900.

MAJOR WORKS

1796-98	LOS CAPRICHOS
1800	CHARLES IV AND THE ROYAL FAMILY
c.1808-12	THE COLOSSUS
c.1810-20	DISASTERS OF WAR
1814	THE SECOND OF MAY, 1808; THE THIRD OF MAY, 1808
c.1820-23	THE "BLACK PAINTINGS"

CASPAR DAVID FRIEDRICH

A serious and solitary figure, Friedrich spent most of his life alone, painting the countryside of his beloved Germany. His mysterious and haunting landscapes expressed not only a love of nature, but also an intense religious belief.

Caspar David Friedrich was born on September 5, 1774, in Greifswald, a town on the German coast. His father, Adolf, was a successful candle and soap maker. He was also a strict Protestant, and led a plain and simple life, avoiding luxury of any kind. This greatly influenced Caspar. Years later, visitors to his home noticed how bare it was.

A TRAGIC CHILDHOOD

Friedrich's childhood was marred by a series of terrible events. He lost his mother in 1781, when he was only seven, and two of his sisters died soon after. The most traumatic experience, however, came in 1787, when his brother drowned trying to rescue him after a skating accident. Caspar felt responsible for the tragedy, and carried the burden of guilt for the rest of his life. This may help explain why he grew into such a gloomy and cheerless adult.

In 1794, Friedrich left his hometown and traveled to the Danish capital, Copenhagen, to study painting. The city's academy was renowned as the best art school in northern Europe. But the young man found its traditional approach restrictive: "All the teaching and instructing kill man's spiritual nature." By now, he had decided to specialize in landscapes.

In 1798, Friedrich moved to Dresden, one of the main art centers in Germany. There, he met a group of artists called the "Dresden Romantics." From his new friends, Friedrich learned about the ideals of Romanticism, a movement that rejected many of the old-fashioned values he had learned at the academy. The Romantics wanted to break away from the art of the past, with its emphasis on order and discipline. Instead, they painted works that were full of drama, emotion, and mystery.

Friedrich learned that his landscapes did not have to be exact copies of

Self-portrait, 1811,
by Caspar David Friedrich
This disturbing picture shows the intense artist when he was 37 years old.

Wanderer looking over a Sea of Fog (detail), c.1815, by Caspar David Friedrich
Standing on a rocky cliff, Friedrich's "wanderer" looks out over a landscape shrouded in thick mists. Absorbed in thought, the figure expresses Friedrich's desire for solitude: "I have to stay alone in order to fully contemplate and feel nature," he wrote.

nature. He realized he could use them to create different moods and feelings, and to display his strong Christian beliefs. "The divine is everywhere," he explained, "even in a grain of sand."

From then on, he produced haunting images of misty sunsets, of ruined chapels half-hidden by gnarled trees, and of strange, motionless figures in moonlight. He often introduced tiny figures into huge panoramas, to emphasize how small and insignificant people were in comparison with the vastness of God's creation. He also used some natural features as symbols, such as a rock standing for unshakeable faith, or an evergreen tree pointing to the eternal hope of the Christian message.

The change in the artist's style may also have been a result of his state of mind. At the time, he was very unhappy, and in 1803, he may have tried to kill himself by cutting his own throat. There were rumors that when he grew a beard after this, it was to hide the scar on his neck. He became a recluse, and gained a reputation as a lonely eccentric.

> "Every true work of art must express a distinct feeling."
> (Friedrich)

Despite these personal difficulties, Friedrich's career was prospering. In 1805, he won an award for one of his paintings. He now began to attract several rich and influential clients.

A CONTROVERSIAL WORK

In 1808, one of his paintings, *The Cross in the Mountains*, became the center of a scandal. He had painted the work—a simple mountain scene with a crucifix at the summit—as an altarpiece for a client's private chapel. When the picture went on show, it horrified many people. Normally, altarpieces featured scenes from the Bible, and the idea of using a landscape—regarded as a minor form of art—seemed like blasphemy.

The publicity probably did Friedrich more good than harm. His works were now selling very well and he was receiving official honors. In 1810, he was made a member of the Berlin Academy and, six years later, he was elected to the academy in Dresden, a post that provided him with a regular income.

With relative financial security came domestic stability. In 1818, at the age of 44, Friedrich married Caroline Bommer, who was less than half his age. Some of his contentment showed in his work. Following the birth of his three children, he painted tender scenes of family life—subjects that would have been unthinkable earlier in his career.

Friedrich's popularity continued to grow during the 1820s, and a group of students and followers gathered around him. Ill health began to catch up with him, however, and in 1825, he suffered a stroke. This did not prevent him from working; some of his greatest pictures date from these final years. Then in 1835, he suffered another, more serious stroke, which left him partly disabled.

By the time Friedrich died in 1840, his art had gone out of fashion. Toward the end of the 19th century, however, a new generation began to recognize his great contribution to German painting.

MAJOR WORKS

1808	THE CROSS IN THE MOUNTAINS
1809	MONK BY THE SEA
c.1815	WANDERER LOOKING OVER A SEA OF FOG
1824	THE ARCTIC SHIPWRECK
c.1835	THE STAGES OF LIFE

J.M.W. TURNER

An intensely private character, Turner used light and color to create atmospheric and imaginative views of nature. Although he attracted much criticism in his day, he is now regarded as one of Britain's greatest artists.

Joseph Mallord William Turner was born on April 23, 1775. His father was a barber, and the family lived above his barber shop in London's Covent Garden, just a few minutes walk from the Thames River. Here, Turner's life-long love of water began.

A TROUBLED CHILDHOOD

Turner's childhood was marred by the ill health of his mother. She suffered from terrible rages and was eventually placed in a lunatic asylum. This must have upset the boy greatly, although he never spoke of it in later life. He was very close to his father, however, who did everything in his power to help him become a painter. He even displayed his son's pictures in his barber shop.

Turner's natural talent shone through at an early age. In 1789, when he was just 14, he attended London's prestigious Royal Academy of Arts. He learned fast, and was soon able to take on a part-time job, making copies of other artists' work for a small fee.

The young artist was soon convinced that his future lay in landscape painting. This meant that he needed to travel, for, while it was possible to earn a modest living painting local scenes, Turner knew that he, like any ambitious artist, needed to portray unusual or dramatic views if he was to make his mark. Such scenes had a wide appeal, because the actual business of traveling was so much harder than it is today. Roads were poor, and the threat of robbery or worse was always present. These dangers were even worse if the traveler ventured abroad.

Turner's first trips were to other parts of Britain. Then, in 1802, he journeyed to France, to see the great collections of art that Napoleon Bonaparte had looted from other parts of Europe. During the same trip, he also traveled to Switzerland to see the breathtaking scenery of the Alps. He

Self-portrait, 1798, by J.M.W. Turner
This rather serious painting shows the ambitious young artist at the age of 23.

made more than 400 sketches of these towering mountains, using them later to help create some of his most impressive and imaginative pictures.

More important still were Turner's tours of Italy, which he visited for the first time in 1819. Here, he was particularly impressed by the warm atmosphere and the hazy quality of the light. In just two months, he made nearly 1,500 sketches in and around Rome.

NEW ROLES

By this time, Turner had already established a firm reputation as a successful artist. In 1802, when he was still only 26, he had been accepted as a full member of the Royal Academy. Five years later, he was made a professor at the school. Teaching does not seem to have been his strong point: Students complained that he mumbled so badly that no one could understand him.

Turner also added a large gallery to his house, where he staged one-man shows of his work. This was an extremely unusual move for an artist, and it demonstrates the great confidence that he felt in his own ability.

A UNIQUE STYLE

Turner's highly original style developed from three main sources. In the first place, he quickly learned the lessons of the great landscape artists of the past, particularly the 17th-century master, Claude Lorrain. Also, Turner shared the fashionable Romantic taste for portraying dramatic scenes of natural disasters. Whirlwinds, avalanches, and raging storms were among his favorite sub-

TURNER'S SEASCAPES

Turner was fascinated by the sea, painting it in all its varied moods and capturing its formidable power.

Early in his career, Turner was influenced by the marine pictures of 17th-century Dutch artists. Their paintings were bold and majestic, and they often paid more attention to the ships than to the sea itself.

Increasingly, however, the artist came under the influence of the Romantics, who regarded nature as a wild, untamed force. This was the aspect of the sea that most interested Turner. He loved painting violent storms and dramatic shipwrecks.

Often, he based such paintings on personal experience. On his first trip to France, his boat was caught in a terrible gale.

jects. These turbulent themes led him to concentrate on the most elusive aspects of a landscape. Increasingly, his interest was drawn away from solid objects, such as buildings and trees, and toward the elements themselves. This fascination with the ingredients of the atmosphere—howling winds, gusts of rain, morning mists—was the third, and most unusual, feature of his work.

Typically, Turner was determined to sketch it, adding the caption "nearly swampt" to his picture.

On another occasion, when Turner was traveling on a steamboat through a storm, he instructed the captain to tie him to the mast so that he could experience the full force of nature at first hand. It is hardly surprising, then, that the churning waves and gusting winds in his seascapes seem so realistic.

Many critics of the time, however, mocked Turner's seascapes, as shown in a cartoon published in 1846 (above). One described his *Snowstorm* as "soapsuds and whitewash."

In seeking to depict these forces of nature, Turner soon learned to apply his paint boldly and freely. He often arranged many of his pictures around a swirling, circular core. This helped to create a sense of energy and movement. He added to this giddying effect by painting in a patch of extremely bright color, which suggested that the viewer was staring into the sun and was half blinded by it. Finally, he deliberately blurred any figures or objects that were featured in the scene.

CAPTURING NATURE

During the 1830s and 1840s, Turner produced some of his most famous works, including *Rain, Steam, and Speed*, exhibited in 1844. This painting reveals his daring approach. A train hurtles across a railroad bridge as rain pounds the scene. The details of the scene are hard to make out; Turner is more concerned with capturing the atmosphere of the moment, rather than depicting every element of the landscape.

In some of his later paintings, the artist went even further in losing the detail, producing pictures that are a blur of colors and shapes. Turner's great rival, the English landscape artist John Constable (*see page 24*), admired this quality, saying Turner seemed to "paint with tinted steam...." Such paintings are very close to abstract art—art that does not represent recognizable objects.

Turner often went to great lengths to capture the color, light, and atmosphere of a scene. A fellow passenger on a train watched with amazement as Turner stuck his head out of a window during a storm. He did so to experience the elements at first hand, in order to paint *Rain, Steam, and Speed*.

STRONG REACTIONS

Some critics were upset by Turner's approach to painting. One complained that Turner's paintings showed "nothing in nature beyond spinach and eggs," while another described his landscapes

The Fighting Temeraire, 1838, by J.M.W. Turner
This painting, one of Turner's most popular works, shows a famous warship being towed up the Thames River to a breaker's yard. The ship in full sail in the background recalls the *Temeraire*'s own days of glory, in contrast to this last, melancholy journey.

as "pictures of nothing." Yet he also had some influential admirers, such as the collector Lord Egremont and the writer and critic John Ruskin.

If criticism bothered Turner, he did not show it. He was a very secretive man and preferred to keep his feelings private. Toward the end of his life, this

to fail. He died in his bedroom overlooking the Thames on December 19, 1851. He was buried with great ceremony in St. Paul's Cathedral in

> "His landscapes
> we could look at
> for ever, though
> there is nothing
> in them."
> (English critic, William
> Hazlitt, 1816)

London. After his funeral, friends were amazed to find more than 300 oil paintings and 20,000 watercolors and drawings rotting away in his studio. In his will, Turner left them to the nation. In 1987, the Tate Gallery in London opened a new wing, the Clore Gallery, to house most of these works.

MAJOR WORKS

1812	HANNIBAL CROSSING THE ALPS
1838	THE FIGHTING TEMERAIRE
C.1840	NORHAM CASTLE: SUNRISE
1842	SNOWSTORM: STEAMBOAT OFF A HARBOR'S MOUTH; PEACE: BURIAL AT SEA
1844	RAIN, STEAM, AND SPEED

habit became more noticeable, and he hardly ever went out or saw people. He bought a new house by the river, building a small gallery in the roof, and lived there with a friend, Sophia Booth, sometimes calling himself "Mr. Booth."

By now, Turner was more than 70 years old, and his health was beginning

JOHN CONSTABLE

Driven by a love of his native southern England, Constable became the greatest painter of the English countryside. But his style of landscape art was unfashionable for much of his lifetime, and he struggled for recognition.

John Constable was born on June 11, 1776, in East Bergholt, a village in Suffolk, southeast England. His father was a prosperous corn merchant. John enjoyed a happy childhood, and he developed a deep, lifelong love for the countryside in which he grew up.

Constable went to a school in nearby Dedham, where a teacher encouraged his interest in drawing. But his real passion for art was born in 1795, when he met Sir George Beaumont, an amateur painter and collector. Beaumont owned a masterpiece by the great 17th-century French landscape painter, Claude Lorrain, which he took with him wherever he went, packed in a special box. The sight of this picture inspired Constable to become an artist.

His father did not approve of the decision, however, knowing that painting was a risky way to earn a living. Instead, he urged his son to join the family business. John obeyed for a time, but he was still desperate to become an artist. In 1799, his father finally allowed him to go to London to study at the Royal Academy of Arts, the most prestigious art school in the country.

THE STUDENT YEARS

Constable was a dedicated student. He spent long evenings drawing. But he was homesick in London, missing his friends, family, and the Suffolk countryside. And he was disappointed to discover that landscape painting, his favorite, was regarded as a low form of art by the academy, which at that time respected history and portrait painting above all. His mother tried to encourage him with letters, and parcels of food.

Constable did not give up, however. He spent his summers back home in Suffolk, using a cottage near his parents' house as a studio in which to paint his landscapes. He also made a number of sketching trips to other parts

John Constable, c.1799, by Ramsay Reinagle
Reinagle painted his friend when they were both students at the Royal Academy.

The Hay Wain, 1821, by John Constable

Constable's most famous work shows an empty hay wagon apparently crossing a river on its way to the meadow beyond. The artist's name for the painting was *Landscape: Noon*. The sun is out of the picture, high in the sky; clouds cast shadows across the green fields.

of the English countryside, to improve his skills as an artist.

By 1809, when he was 33, Constable had more or less mastered his craft. But he had not yet made a success of his career. While the dramatic and imaginative scenes of his fellow student at the academy, J.M.W. Turner (*see page 18*), sold very well, Constable found it hard to sell his work because people thought it ordinary and uninteresting.

In addition, Constable had not yet been elected as a member of the Royal Academy, which was vital if he was to be a successful artist. The contrast between his career and that of Turner could not have been greater. Turner was elected a full member of the academy

at the age of 26. He dominated landscape art, with his work commanding high prices. Constable, on the other hand, was 39 years old before he sold his first painting.

At this unpromising point, Constable fell in love with Maria Bicknell, the daughter of a wealthy civil servant. Maria's family opposed her romance with a poor artist, and threatened to disinherit her if she married him. This unhappy situation continued for the next seven years, during which time the couple were often apart. They remained loyal to each other, however.

Constable's stubborn personality helped him to survive this difficult period. Although he sometimes suffered bouts of depression, he forced himself to follow a strict work routine. He spent his summers at East Bergholt, sketching from nature, and his winters in London, working his sketches into large paintings. In this way, he gradually developed his own unique landscape style.

At the time, it was still common for artists to paint entire landscapes inside their studios. They would work from memory, making sure that the colors were attractive and the composition balanced. They did not worry too much about accuracy. Constable rejected this method. He wanted his pictures to look real, reflecting every movement of a cloud, every change in the weather. "No two days are alike," he wrote, "nor even two hours; neither were there ever two leaves of a tree alike since the creation of the world." A fellow painter once said that Constable's rainy landscapes looked so realistic that they made him want to reach for his coat and umbrella.

MARRIAGE AND SUCCESS

In 1816, Constable's father died, leaving him some money in his will. This freed John and Maria to marry. The wedding took place on October 2, 1816—none of Maria's family attended the ceremony. The newlyweds moved to a house in north London, and the first of their seven children was born in 1817.

Marriage filled Constable with renewed inspiration, and he began work on several huge paintings of the Suffolk countryside that were to become his best-loved masterpieces. In 1821, he painted *The Hay Wain*, now the most famous of them all. This tranquil scene

of a farm cart crossing a river brought Constable recognition. When it went on show in France in 1824, the French king honored the painter with a gold medal.

Just as success seemed assured, tragedy struck. Maria developed a lung disease, which eventually killed her in 1828. Constable was heartbroken, but he continued working. In 1829, at the age of 53, he was finally elected a member of the Royal Academy, by just one vote. His rival Turner came to deliver the news in person, staying to talk with Constable late into the night.

This recognition of Constable's talent came too late to influence his career—his most creative years had passed. Six years later, in 1835, he produced his last major picture of Suffolk, *The Valley Farm*. He told the buyer that he had painted the work "for a very particular person … the person for whom I have painted all my life." Constable was not to be apart from his beloved Maria for much longer. He died on March 31, 1837, and was buried alongside her.

MAJOR WORKS	
1815	BOATBUILDING
1817	FLATFORD MILL
1821	THE HAY WAIN
1823	SALISBURY CATHEDRAL
1826	THE CORNFIELD
1835	THE VALLEY FARM
1836	STONEHENGE

EUGÈNE DELACROIX

Passionate and uncompromising, Delacroix became the leader of the Romantic movement in art with energetic and boldly colored works that shocked the public and critics alike.

Ferdinand Victor Eugène Delacroix was born in a suburb of Paris on April 26, 1798. His father had been a member of the government at the time of the French Revolution. But there were rumors that Eugène's mother had been the mistress of Charles Talleyrand, an important politician of the time, and that the boy was really his son.

AN EVENTFUL CHILDHOOD

Eugène was a lively child. His friend, the writer Alexandre Dumas, recalled that "by the age of three, he had been hanged, burned, drowned, and choked." He was "hanged" when he trapped his head in a horse's feed bag; "burned" when a mosquito net over his bed caught fire; "drowned" when a servant dropped him in a harbor; and "choked" when swallowing a grape.

More seriously, Delacroix's childhood was upset by the early death of both his parents. As a result, he was sent to live with his older sister in 1814. Eugène was still unclear where his future lay, but his love of sketching, which had developed during vacations in Normandy, helped him make up his mind. In 1815, he became a student of Pierre-Narcisse Guérin, one of the leading painters of the day, before moving to the School of Fine Arts in Paris a year later.

NEOCLASSICISM

At the time, the Neoclassical style of painting was very popular. Neoclassical artists modeled their work on the art of ancient Greece and Rome. Their training was based around a strict program of careful drawing and the study of antique sculpture, and they took their subjects from history or mythology.

Delacroix certainly saw drawing as an essential skill. He often did hundreds of sketches before beginning a large picture. He also declared that it was

Self-portrait, c.1818, by Eugène Delacroix **This picture shows Delacroix around the age of 20. He said of the work, "The wickedness of my expression ... frightens me."**

impossible for a person to become a great artist if he or she were "not skillful enough to sketch a man falling out of a window, during the time it takes him to get from the fifth floor to the ground."

But this speed and power of observation were not the sort of talents that appealed to Neoclassical critics. They preferred drawing to be careful and detailed, with the artist copying every hair on the model's head.

SENSATIONAL ART

This methodical approach was not in Delacroix's nature. Passion and drama were at the heart of his work. This is obvious from his reaction to *The Raft of the Medusa*, a stirring shipwreck scene by a fellow student, Théodore Géricault. Delacroix was so excited that, after leaving his friend's studio, "he started running like a madman," not stopping until he reached his own room.

Géricault's painting provided the inspiration for *The Barque of Dante*, Delacroix's first major canvas. In 1822, it was shown at the Salon—the official exhibit staged by the French state. It caused a sensation. Baron Gros, one of the most popular artists of the time, hailed it as "a subdued Rubens," referring to the 17th-century Flemish painter.

Leaving art school in triumph, Delacroix threw himself into the burning artistic debates of the day. Within just a few years, he established himself as a leading figure in the Romantic movement, the new style which had developed in opposition to Neoclassicism. As such, he suddenly found that his pictures attracted a storm of criticism. This

DELACROIX AND COLOR

Color was Delacroix's great obsession. He developed an influential way of making his colors more intense.

Early on in his career, Delacroix realized that color was the key to his art: It would allow him to fill his pictures with a heightened sense of drama and emotion.

This belief was strengthened one day, when he saw a bright ray of sunshine light up a carriage, casting violet shadows on the ground beneath. The yellow of the carriage suddenly seemed particularly intense. Delacroix realized that this was because the two contrasting tones appeared side by side. Immediately, he tried to create the same effect on canvas.

Instead of mixing his paints to produce a single, bright color, he

was particularly true of his two masterpieces of the 1820s, *The Massacre of Chios* and *The Death of Sardanapalus*.

The criticism centered around two main issues. The supporters of Neoclassicism disapproved of Delacroix's lively, fluid style, which failed to include every small detail of the scene. They even believed that his pictures were only sketches, and were not finished.

placed two unmixed patches of "complementary" colors next to each other. Each of the three primary colors—red, blue, and yellow—has a complementary color, as shown in Delacroix's color triangle (*above*). This is created by a mixture of the other two. Green, for example—formed by a mixture of blue and yellow—is the complementary of red, and reveals its true vibrancy. Delacroix's use of color influenced later painters, particularly the Impressionists, who flourished toward the end of the 19th century.

The same critics also found the subjects of his paintings distasteful. Neoclassical pictures traditionally upheld certain values. Their subjects were meant to be drawn from the past, and their moods were supposed to be noble, heroic, and highly moral.

Delacroix's first painting had been acceptable, because it had been about Dante, an early Italian poet. But his later works were controversial. *The Massacre of Chios* raised eyebrows because it was about a modern event—a tragic episode in the Greek War of Independence. Most people thought that this type of subject was more appropriate for a journalist than for an artist.

TASTE FOR THE EXOTIC

Similarly, in *The Death of Sardanapalus*, Delacroix dealt with material by a modern writer, Lord Byron (*see page 38*). Here, the artist's opponents were appalled at the way he seemed to take great pleasure in focusing on images of violence and cruelty. This taste for the wild and the exotic, however, was common to most of the Romantics.

> "A volcanic crater artistically concealed beneath bouquets of flowers."
> (Charles Baudelaire on Delacroix)

In 1832, Delacroix got the chance to study the exotic at first hand when he joined an official state visit to the sultan of Morocco. He stayed for six weeks in Tangier, North Africa, and then journeyed 200 miles to the sultan's palace. There, the French party were given a number of unusual gifts: a lion, a tiger, Arabian horses, and gazelles.

At the time, travel was still quite difficult and very few Europeans managed

Algerian Women in their Apartment, 1834, by Eugène Delacroix
**This typically exotic subject reveals Delacroix's love of rich color and sensuous detail.
He uses complementary colors to create a vibrant color harmony. To the right, for example,
a brilliant strand of green in the woman's turban brings out the intensity of the red material.**

to travel to Africa. Not surprisingly, Delacroix was amazed by the strange and wonderful sights that he saw on his trip. "In this short time," he remarked, "I have lived through 20 times as much as in months spent in Paris."

The artist's memories and the hundreds of sketches he made were to inspire him for the rest of his life. He painted a variety of Arabian scenes and, remembering how vivid everything had seemed under the African sun, he also tried to enrich the colors in his pictures.

By the mid-1830s, the fiercest arguments about Romanticism were over, and Delacroix's talents became recognized more widely. As a result, the authorities began to shower him with offers to paint large-scale murals on the walls and ceilings of public buildings and churches in Paris.

Every ambitious artist wanted to be given work of this kind. It was well paid and, more importantly, it showed that he had reached the top of his profession: Only artists of the highest quality were honored with these important public contracts.

The disadvantage of such jobs was that they required years of patient and continuous effort. It took Delacroix 14 years to complete the murals in the Bourbon Palace—1833 to 1847—and a further eight to decorate the church of Saint-Sulpice—1853 to 1861.

During this time, he had to make endless sketches and cover huge areas of space. As a friend wrote: "To imagine

> "One must be bold to extremity; without daring, and even extreme daring, there is no beauty."
> (Eugène Delacroix)

what such labor was like, you had to have seen him at the end of the day … pale, tired out, hardly able to talk, dragging himself along as if he'd just escaped from torture."

These exhausting chores affected the artist's social life. For years, Delacroix had been welcome in the houses of the rich and famous, where his wit and sparkling company were in demand. But as he reached middle age, he began to avoid these fashionable gatherings. He had only a few real friends, among them the Polish composer, Frédéric Chopin (*see page 76*), and the French novelist, George Sand. By 1844, he was

also renting a house near Fontaine-bleau, around 30 miles south of Paris, to give him some peace from the bustle of the capital.

HONORS AT LAST

In 1855, there was a major exhibit of Delacroix's paintings, acknowledging his lifetime of achievement. He was awarded the Grand Medal of Honor, and created a Commander of the Legion of Honor. Two years later, he was finally elected to the Academy of Fine Arts.

Although he was grateful for this recognition, Delacroix was disappointed to find that his newer work met with indifference. The critics attacked the pictures that he exhibited at the Salon of 1859. With great sorrow, the artist decided that he would send no more. Worse still, his completion in 1861 of the murals at Saint-Sulpice passed almost unnoticed. After this, Delacroix became a virtual recluse in his Paris apartment. He died on August 13, 1863, a sad and forgotten figure.

MAJOR WORKS

1822	THE BARQUE OF DANTE
1824	THE MASSACRE OF CHIOS
1827	THE DEATH OF SARDANAPALUS
1830	LIBERTY LEADING THE PEOPLE
1834	ALGERIAN WOMEN
1853-61	MURALS AT CHURCH OF SAINT-SULPICE

WILLIAM WORDSWORTH

Generally acknowledged as the father of Romantic poetry, Wordsworth spent his life quietly in the English Lake District, writing passionate poetry inspired by the beautiful and lonely countryside.

Williaim Wordsworth was born on April 7, 1770, at Cockermouth, a small market town on the edge of the Lake District in northwest England. He was the second son of John, a lawyer, and Anne, who died when William was eight. He did not enjoy school and learned little. He preferred to wander alone in the isolated and windswept hills of the local countryside.

John Wordsworth died in 1783, leaving William and his three brothers and one sister in the care of relatives. When William was 17 years old, his guardians scraped together enough money to send him to Cambridge University. But he soon grew bored with student life and neglected his studies.

A REVOLUTIONARY ZEAL

In 1790, while he should have been studying, Wordsworth traveled with a friend to Switzerland and France. He was fired by enthusiasm for the ideals of the French Revolution, which had begun the previous year.

After graduating, Wordsworth spent some months in London—which he hated—before returning to France in 1791. He strongly supported the new republic, and considered finding a job in its government. He fell in love with a girl named Annette Vallon, who bore him a daughter. He left for England to raise money, perhaps intending to go back and marry Annette, but war broke out between Britain and France, ending the relationship.

This romantic trauma may have prompted Wordsworth to begin writing. Before long, he had published his first poems. They aroused little interest, however. Their formal and artificial style, inspired by classical poetry, seemed old-fashioned to many.

At this time, Wordsworth was very short of money. Despite his financial problems, his relatives refused to help:

William Wordsworth, 1842,
by Benjamin Haydon
This portrait shows the poet at the age of 72, in his beloved Lake District.

A view of the Lake District, by Samuel Jackson

A magnificent mountain or lake scene like this one could provoke an ecstatic vision in Wordsworth's mind. The poet described one such occasion in *The Prelude*: "And I have felt / A presence that disturbs me with joy / Of elevated thoughts; a sense sublime ...."

they were annoyed that he did not have a "proper" career. Then, in 1795, came a turning point in his fortunes. A friend died and left him a large sum of money. This windfall was enough to support him for the next eight years, and allowed him to look after his sister, Dorothy, who now shared his home and was his closest companion.

COLLABORATION

In 1795, William and Dorothy moved to Somerset, southwest England, becoming neighbors of the poet, Samuel Taylor Coleridge. The two young writers stimulated each other to an intense pitch of creativity. Coleridge described himself, William, and Dorothy as "three people, but only one soul."

In 1798, the three friends decided to travel to Germany. To help finance the trip, Wordsworth and Coleridge published *Lyrical Ballads*, a collection of their poems.

The work showed a radical departure from contemporary poetry, not only in its freshness of language, but also in the way it associated forms in nature with human emotions. In a preface to the volume, Wordsworth—who had written 19 out of the 23 poems—explained that his intention was to choose "situations from common life, and to relate or describe them ... in a language really used by men."

The collection contained several masterpieces, and has since been acknowledged as the starting point of the Romantic movement. But at the time, it received just three reviews, and sold only a handful of copies. In fact, the publisher was so disappointed by the slow sales that he gave the rights to the volume back to Wordsworth, who was then able to bring out later editions.

A RETURN TO THE LAKES

William and Dorothy returned from Germany in February 1799, and rented a small house called Dove Cottage in Grasmere, a village in the Lake District. In 1802, Wordsworth married his cousin, Mary Hutchinson. Mary settled well into the close-knit household, and the couple had five children.

During his time at Dove Cottage, Wordsworth reached his creative peak. He wrote with a stubborn dedication, constantly revising his work, and having little time to do other things.

His main source of inspiration came from the countryside of his beloved Lake District. In his poems, he not only described the natural scenes he saw, but also spoke of a close, spiritual link between humans and nature. For Wordsworth, like the later Romantics, the city spelled confusion, corruption, and false values. It was only by being alone in nature—in its various moods, from gentle to wild and sublime—that an individual could find truth and beauty.

Wordsworth's poetry was much admired by his small circle of friends, and word of his talent soon spread. His inspiration diminished as his reputation grew, however. As he got older, he also became more conservative, abandoning the revolutionary ideals of his youth.

This led to attacks from younger Romantic poets, such as Lord Byron (*see page 38*) and Percy Bysshe Shelley. Nonetheless, many people still thought Wordsworth's poetry too radical. His earnings remained pitifully small.

In 1813, he became distributor of government revenue stamps in his local area. The post made him a wealthy man. He moved into his last and grandest home, Rydal Mount. He was also able to travel, which inspired him to recapture flashes of his youthful brilliance.

LATE HONOR

By 1830, Romantic poetry had become increasingly popular, and the 60-year-old Wordsworth was now one of England's most famous writers. In 1843, he reached the pinnacle of his career when Queen Victoria made him poet laureate—the official royal poet.

The loss of his daughter Dorothy in 1847 darkened Wordsworth's remaining years. He died three years after her, on April 23, 1850. A few months later, Mary published the most ambitious of all her husband's works—*The Prelude*—which Wordsworth had completed back in 1805, but had revised many times over.

MAJOR WORKS	
1793	DESCRIPTIVE SKETCHES
1798	LYRICAL BALLADS
1807	POEMS IN TWO VOLUMES
1814	THE EXCURSION
1850	THE PRELUDE

LORD BYRON

Famous not only as a poet, but also as a handsome, dashing, and rebellious personality, Byron lived life to the full. His many romances and adventures helped shape the image of the Romantic hero.

George Gordon, Lord Byron, was born in London on January 22, 1788. Soon after, his parents, Catherine and John, fled to Scotland to escape creditors. In 1791, John—who had been married once before, and had a daughter, Augusta—died. George's mother was left to bring the boy up on her own.

THE LIFE OF A LORD

In 1798, Byron became the sixth Lord Byron when his great-uncle died. Along with his title, the young man inherited Newstead Abbey, an estate near Nottingham, in the heart of England.

The teenage Byron went to boarding school at Harrow, near London. He was a lazy pupil, although very intelligent. He was also an active sportsman, despite a deformed and lame foot. In 1805, he went to Cambridge University. He received his degree three years later.

Byron was a typical young aristocrat—good-looking and fashionable, deeply in debt, and rebellious. Unlike most young lords, however, in 1807 he published a volume of verse, *Hours of Idleness*. When the *Edinburgh Review* attacked the book, Byron replied with a satirical poem, *English Bards and Scotch Reviewers*, in which he attacked the *Review*'s editor. He also criticized the leading Romantic writers, such as William Wordsworth (*see page 34*).

In 1809, Byron left England on a tour of the Mediterranean. He fell in love with Greece. "If I am a poet," he said later, "the air of Greece has made me one." Byron returned home penniless.

In March 1812, Byron had his first literary success with the first two cantos—or sections—of a poem called *Childe Harold's Pilgrimage*, the story of a man who gives up a life of pleasure to travel around the Mediterranean. The poem's first edition sold out almost immediately. Byron "woke up one morning and found [myself] famous."

Lord Byron, 1813, by Thomas Phillips
This dark and atmospheric portrait shows the handsome and charismatic poet at the age of 21.

The poem introduced a new kind of hero—a thoughtful yet defiant outcast. Contemporaries assumed the figure was based on the poet himself, which added to the public's fascination with Byron. The poet was in great demand in fashionable circles. In particular, women found him captivating: One called him "mad, bad, and dangerous to know." Byron lived up to his reputation: Throughout his life, he had affairs with many women, including the novelist Lady Caroline Lamb, and, according to rumor, even his own half sister, Augusta.

During the following years, Byron wrote *The Giaour*, *The Corsair*, and other similar narrative poems. Their exotic eastern settings and mysterious, tormented heroes reinforced the Byronic image. They were all very popular. Byron claimed that 14,000 copies of *The Corsair* were sold in a single day.

Byron's life then seemed to become more stable. Early in 1815, he married Annabella Milbanke, and the couple had a daughter. Yet the marriage ended after only 15 months. By now, Byron was becoming notorious. His debts were rising, and people around him questioned his sanity. Those who had once admired him now scorned him.

A LIFE IN EXILE

On April 24, 1816, Byron left England forever, and went to Switzerland. There he met up with an old friend, Claire Clairmont. She introduced him to her stepsister, Mary Shelley (*see page 46*), and to Mary's husband, the poet Percy Bysshe Shelley. The two poets became friends, living at Lake Geneva. Here,

BYRON'S DON JUAN

In the summer of 1818, Byron began *Don Juan*, a long, epic poem about the adventures of a young hero.

Byron's masterpiece, *Don Juan*, is a mix of satire, farce, passion, and social comment. The poem tells the story of a passionate and lively young man's journey through life. Aristocratic, proud, and immoral, he stands on the edges of society, forever condemned to remain an outsider. Wherever he visits—Greece, Turkey, Russia, and England—the handsome Spaniard falls in love with beautiful women, but he never feels at home.

In many ways, *Don Juan* is an autobiographical work, whose appeal lay partly in the public's fascination with Lord Byron himself. The bold and dashing

Byron completed the third canto of *Childe Harold*. After Shelley returned to England, Byron settled in Venice. He sold Newstead Abbey to clear his debts, and lived from his writing.

In the summer of 1818, Byron began writing *Don Juan*. Early reviewers condemned the first two cantos as "filthy and impious." Byron even considered quitting. But the public loved the

Don Juan (*above*) was a new kind of hero. Although he is immoral, he is an immensely likable character. Byron himself best described the contradictions in his work: "Confess, confess, you dog—it may be bawdy, but is it not good English? It may be profligate, but is it not life, is it not the thing?"

Byron used an informal, conversational style for *Don Juan*. This enabled him to discuss a range of subjects, from history and current affairs to philosophy. The poem is a comedy about society in general.

poem, and so Byron added further cantos: At the time of his death, he had begun the seventeenth.

In England, meanwhile, Claire had given birth to Byron's daughter, Allegra. Byron put the child in a convent, but at the age of five, she died of typhus. The poet was heartbroken, and never spoke her name again. Byron and Claire's relationship ended soon afterward.

In 1819, Byron left Venice for Ravenna, northern Italy, where he continued to write. For several years, he led a relatively settled life. But the political situation in Italy was changing. The country was dominated by the Austrian Hapsburg dynasty. Many Italians were discontented with their rulers, and secret movements began to promote the republican cause. Byron sympathized with these ideals and launched a republican newspaper, *The Liberal*, with Shelley. But in 1822, Shelley drowned off the northwestern coast of Italy; his death marked the end of the project.

By 1823, Byron had become obsessed with the Greek struggle for independence from Turkey, which had started in 1821. He went to fight, telling a friend before he left, "I have a presentiment I shall die in Greece."

In January 1824, Byron was at Missolonghi, helping train the Greek troops. Missolonghi was a marshy area where malaria flourished. On April 9, Byron fell ill with a fever. After nine days, he murmured: "Now I shall go to sleep." He died the following evening. His body was taken back to England and buried near his old home, Newstead Abbey.

MAJOR WORKS

1807	HOURS OF IDLENESS
1809	ENGLISH BARDS AND SCOTCH REVIEWERS
1812-17	CHILDE HAROLD'S PILGRIMAGE
1818-24	DON JUAN

JOHN KEATS

Although he died at the age of just 26, Keats left a remarkable body of work. He suffered savage criticism of his poetry, as well as the constant pain of his fatal illness, yet his odes are among literature's highlights.

John Keats was born on October 31, 1795. His early childhood was comfortable and happy. His father, Thomas, ran a successful livery stable—where horses are kept and fed for their owners—and sent John and his two elder brothers, Tom and George, to a good school north of London. There, John developed an interest in classical mythology and medieval folklore. But the happy family was shattered when Thomas fell from his horse and died. Five years later, John's mother also died. From then on, guardians cared for the orphaned Keats children.

FROM DOCTOR TO POET

One of these guardians arranged for Keats to be apprenticed to a surgeon and apothecary, or pharmacist. The young man eventually qualified as a doctor in 1816, and spent a few months practicing surgery in a London hospital. But his heart was not in it: Already Keats was more interested in writing poetry than in a medical career.

Poetry soon became the dominant force in Keats's life. The year he qualified, he met Leigh Hunt, a well-known writer. Hunt was a central member of a group of young artists and writers that included the English poet Percy Bysshe Shelley. Hunt was impressed by Keats's poetry, and published the young poet's "To Solitude" in his literary magazine, *The Examiner*.

PUBLISHING HIS POETRY

Keats now began to divide his time between the London house he shared with his brothers and Hunt's cottage in Hampstead. In 1817, with the help of some technical advice from Shelley, he published his first collection of work, *Poems*. The critics ignored it.

Keats was not discouraged, however, and went on to write *Endymion: a Poetic Romance* in 1818, which con-

John Keats, 1819, by William Hutton after Joseph Severn
This portrait shows the serious young poet at the age of 24—two years before he died.

tains one of poetry's best-loved lines: "A thing of beauty is a joy forever." Some critics savagely attacked the work, however; one review sneered: "It is better to be a starved apothecary than a starved poet; so back to the shop Mr. John, back to the 'plasters, pills, and ointment boxes.'"

TRAVEL AND TRAGEDY

The poet traveled outside of southern England for the first time in 1818, going on a walking tour around England and Scotland. He enjoyed the scenery. Unlike most of the Romantic poets, however, Keats's interest in nature was limited; he was more concerned with humankind. "Scenery is fine," he said, "but human nature is finer."

Shelley would later maintain that it was the cruel attacks of the critics that broke Keats's heart and caused his early death. In fact, there was a more medical explanation. It was during his walking tour that Keats showed the first symptoms of tuberculosis—a disease that affects the lungs. Upon Keats's return to London, his brother Tom died from the disease. It would eventually kill Keats himself.

LOVE AND CREATIVITY

After Tom's death, Keats moved to another part of London, where he met a young neighbor, Fanny Brawne. He fell in love with her immediately. He wrote her many passionate poems and letters. The couple became engaged secretly in 1819.

During this time, Keats also enjoyed a period of great creativity: He wrote

---

KEATS'S ODES

An ode is a poem written to celebrate a person or thing. Keats brought this type of poem to great heights.

Keats's odes are considered by many to be among the finest short poems in English. Like the poems of Shelley and Byron, Keats's works have the Romantic qualities of intensity of vision, freshness of language, and emphasis on personal experience.

One theme common to all Keats's odes is the contradiction between permanence and mortality: while some things remain, humankind will always face death. In "Ode on a Grecian Urn," the urn—a symbol of permanence—is contrasted with human transience, or impermanence: "When old age shall this generation waste / Thou shalt remain."

---

many of his most famous odes between 1818 and 1819. Curiously, however, he seems to have considered many of these to be unimportant. He presented "La Belle Dame sans Merci" to his brother George very casually. And "Ode to a Nightingale"—which he wrote within a few hours—only survived because a friend persuaded him to keep it rather than throw it away.

In "Ode to a Nightingale" (*above*), Keats yearns to be free from the real world of pain, decay, and death, to enjoy the freedom of a bird. He sees that he must accept life as it is, saying "'Beauty is truth, truth beauty' — that is all / Ye know on earth, and all ye need to know."

Toward the end of 1819, Keats became very ill and started to cough up blood. He knew from his medical training that he had tuberculosis: "I know the color of that blood … I cannot be deceived …; that drop of blood is my death warrant." His illness also caused him emotional pain, as he realized that he would not have a future life with Fanny. Their relationship was stormy,

and a friend who visited him noted that he had "lost his cheerfulness." Sometimes, the poet resorted to drugs to ease his constant pain.

Nevertheless, in the summer of 1820, Keats played a small part in overseeing the publication of a volume of his poetry. It gained a surprisingly good reception, even from some journals that had formerly been hostile to him.

AN EARLY DEATH

This success came just as the poet's health took a turn for the worse. In late 1820, Keats's doctor advised him that only the sun of southern Europe might cure him. He decided to join Shelley in Italy. His good friend, the painter Joseph Severn, went with him.

On arriving in Rome, the men took rooms in the center of the city. Here, Keats spent the last three months of his life, reading and playing the piano. During this time, he was all too aware of his impending death, feeling "the flowers growing over me." After terrible suffering, Keats died on February 23, 1821, and was buried in Rome.

MAJOR WORKS

1817	POEMS
1818	ENDYMION: A POETIC ROMANCE; ISABELLA, OR THE POT OF BASIL
1819	"ODE TO A NIGHTINGALE;" "ODE TO MELANCHOLY;" "ODE ON A GRECIAN URN;" "ODE TO PSYCHE;" "ODE TO AUTUMN"

MARY SHELLEY

The tale of Frankenstein, which inspires horror movies to this day, was the startling achievement of a modest young woman. It brought Mary Shelley fame—matching that of her celebrated husband—but not happiness.

Mary Shelley was born in London on August 30, 1797, to the feminist pioneer Mary Wollstonecraft and the political philosopher William Godwin. Her mother died just ten days after her birth. Godwin remarried a few years later, and the family lived over a store in central London. It was here that Mary first met Percy Bysshe Shelley, the man who was to change her life.

A SECRET AFFAIR

Shelley was an aristocrat, a poet, and a political revolutionary. He had married at 19, but his marriage had fallen apart. He often visited Godwin to talk about philosophy, and he soon fell in love with the 16-year-old Mary.

When Mary's father discovered the secret romance, he was horrified. So, in June 1814, the couple ran away. They took Mary's stepsister, Jane, with them and fled first to France, then Switzerland. They quickly ran out of money, however, and when Mary became pregnant, they decided to return to England.

Plagued by financial problems, Mary gave birth prematurely to a daughter, who died two weeks later. Mary's despair at the baby's death was made worse when she realized that Shelley was now more interested in her stepsister than he was in her. Jane, who now called herself Claire, soon left their household, however. Mary became pregnant again, and she settled down to a peaceful, domestic life with Shelley. The couple had a healthy son, William, in January 1816.

By this time, Claire had become involved with the poet Lord Byron (*see page 38*), and persuaded Mary and Shelley to travel with her to Switzerland. They joined Byron on the shores of Lake Geneva and spent the summer boating and talking into the night at Byron's villa. They passed the time making up ghost stories, which

Mary Shelley, 1840, by Richard Rothwell
Rothwell's portrait shows Shelley in middle age. By this time, the famous, but tragic, novelist had given up writing fiction.

became the starting point of Mary's first novel—the horror story, *Frankenstein*.

Mary and Shelley returned to England in September 1816, moving to Bath, in the southwest of the country. A few months later, they heard that Shelley's wife, Harriet, had killed herself. Shelley rushed back to London to claim custody of his and Harriet's two children, while Mary—pregnant once more—stayed behind to finish *Frankenstein*. To give Shelley a greater chance of gaining custody of the children, he and Mary married in December 1816.

FAME AND TRAGEDY

In March 1818, the Shelleys traveled to Tuscany, central Italy with their children—Mary had given birth to a daughter, Clara, in 1817—and Mary's stepsister Claire. Meanwhile, *Frankenstein* had been published anonymously, and Mary was getting reports of its reception.

The book was selling very well, despite shocking its readers and receiving mixed reviews. Although it contained many elements of the fashionable Gothic novel, it made none of the customary moral statements about good and evil. Some critics attacked the work's "horrible and disgusting absurdity," but others praised the author's "original genius and happy power of expression." Most assumed that Percy Bysshe Shelley had written the book. They were astounded to learn that its author was in fact Mary.

In August 1818, Shelley and Claire visited Byron in Venice, northern Italy, and later asked Mary to join them. Although Clara was sick, Mary set out.

SHELLEY'S FRANKENSTEIN

One of the most famous horror stories, *Frankenstein* satisfied the 19th-century taste for the macabre.

Shelley's tale of terror relates the exploits of Victor Frankenstein (*right*), a young Swiss nobleman who discovers the secret of life. Frankenstein collects bodies, and builds a huge, superstrong creature. At first, the monster is kind and gentle, and seeks human company, but its appearance is so hideous that it terrifies everyone, including Frankenstein.

The lonely monster begs Victor to build it a mate. When Frankenstein refuses, it kills its creator's bride and his best friend, and escapes to the Arctic. Frankenstein follows it, but dies in the pursuit. The monster then disappears to end its own life.

The baby died on the journey—Mary always blamed Shelley for the tragedy.

The party made a trip to Rome—Mary's favorite city. But she could not shake off her sense of gloom. In 1819, her son William got dysentery, and died two weeks later. His loss marked Mary for life. Unconsoled by becoming pregnant again, she rushed to Tuscany, on the verge of a nervous breakdown.

In July 1822, Shelley and Williams took a sailing trip up the Italian coast to Livorno. Mary had begged them not to go, writing that she felt "a vague expectation of evil." The men arrived safely, but on the return voyage their boat sank in a storm. Ten days later, their bodies were washed up.

LIFE WITHOUT SHELLEY

Grief-stricken, Mary longed to die, but her son needed her. She pulled herself together, planning to stay in Italy and write. But when her husband's family refused to help her unless she gave up the baby, Mary returned to England.

When *Valperga* was published in 1823, it sold as well as *Frankenstein* had done. Mary gave all the profits to her penniless father. Her third novel, however, *The Last Man*, was not as successful: tastes had changed. For her next work, *Lodore*, published in 1835, Mary altered her style. Instead of a highly imaginative story, she wrote a society novel, filled with episodes and characters from her own life. *Lodore* was a success—but it was to be her last. In the final 15 years of her life, Mary wrote no more fiction. She died on February 1, 1851.

Frankenstein is perhaps the best-known example of the Gothic novel. These chilling horror stories thrilled readers in England and America in the late 18th and early 19th centuries. They had eerie settings, such as gloomy castles or ruined, moonlit monasteries, and spooky props, such as cobwebs, flickering candles, lightning, and skeletons.

Mary had a son, Percy, in November 1819, but she doubted that he would live. To add to her worries, her father was demanding money from her, and her relations with Claire were strained. Eventually, Claire left, and Mary settled down to write *Valperga*, a medieval romance. In 1820, the Shelleys moved to Pisa, where they made new friends, including Edward and Jane Williams.

MAJOR WORKS

1818	FRANKENSTEIN
1823	VALPERGA
1826	THE LAST MAN
1835	LODORE

VICTOR HUGO

A dynamic personality, Victor Hugo's novels, poetry, and plays dominated French literature for over 50 years. In the course of his life, he was a politician, an exile in the name of freedom, and a national hero.

Victor Hugo was born on February 26, 1802, in Besançon, a town in eastern France. His father, Joseph, was a general in the French army. He was a distant figure for Victor and his two older brothers, since he lived abroad for most of their childhood. The boys lived in Paris with their mother, Sophie, who had left Joseph shortly after Victor's birth.

EARLY SUCCESS

Victor's talent for poetry flowered early. When he was 15, he was honored by the French Academy, and a year later he won his first poetry competition. His first volume of poetry, *Odes et poésies diverses—Odes and other poems—*was published in 1822, when he was just 20. It was well received, and the young poet was awarded a royal pension. This gave him a regular income, allowing him to marry his childhood sweetheart, Adèle.

But 1822 was a year of tragedy as well as success for Hugo. His mother died, and his brother, Eugène, who was secretly in love with Adèle, went insane

at Hugo's wedding. The writer endured these traumas bravely, showing the strength of character which would help him in a life filled with tragedies.

A ROMANTIC SPOKESMAN

By 1830, the couple had four children. Hugo's huge appetite for work enabled him to support his family in style. He became leader of the French Romantics —a group of artists and writers who, like the Romantics in England and Germany, argued against the strict rules of classical art and literature. Hugo believed that these rules hindered expressive, imaginative writing. His 1829 book of poetry, *Les Orientales—The Oriental Women*—won him many supporters.

Hugo's dispute with the Classicists climaxed in 1830, with the production of his play, *Hernani*. It became known as the "battle of *Hernani*," since the

Victor Hugo
This undated photograph shows the French writer in a somber mood, probably during his period of exile on Guernsey.

actors could hardly be heard above the hisses and cheers of rival groups in the audience. By the end of the play's run, however, Romanticism had emerged victorious, and Hugo was hailed as the leading French writer of his generation.

Success inflated Hugo's already large ego. Adèle could not bear his arrogance, and by the end of 1830, she was having an affair with another man. Hugo was distraught, but continued to produce great literature throughout the 1830s. In 1831, *Notre-Dame de Paris*—known as *The Hunchback of Notre-Dame*—raised him to new heights of popularity.

POLITICS AND EXILE

As Hugo grew older, he became more and more interested in politics. In 1845, he was made a nobleman, which meant he could enter the French parliament. Here, he campaigned passionately on behalf of the poor and oppressed.

In 1848, revolution broke out in France. The king fled the country, and the French people proclaimed a republic. Hugo was elected as a deputy to the new National Assembly, and formed a magazine, *L'Événement—The Event*— as a mouthpiece for his radical ideas.

The first president of the republic, Louis Napoleon, was the nephew of Napoleon Bonaparte, the emperor of France between 1804 and 1814. At first, Hugo supported Louis Napoleon.

Once in power, however, the new president passed strict laws limiting freedom of speech. By 1851, Hugo hated him. The writer criticized Louis Napoleon in *L'Événement*, and taunted him in the National Assembly with the

HUGO'S HUNCHBACK

Hugo's moving tale of the hunchback of Notre-Dame has captivated generations of readers.

Set in 15th-century Paris, Hugo's tale tells the story of Quasimodo, the deformed bellringer of Notre-Dame Cathedral. He falls in love with Esmeralda, a gypsy girl, and foolishly tries to kidnap her. For his crime, he is put in the pillory, whipped, and pelted with rocks. In the middle of his agony, Esmeralda, having forgiven him, tenderly gives him some water (*right*).

Later, Esmeralda is wrongly accused of murder and sentenced to death. Quasimodo shows his love and gratitude by swinging down from his belfry and carrying her away as she is about to be executed. By portraying the hunchback as a good

famous line, "Because we have had a Napoleon the Great, must we have a Napoleon the Little?"

In December 1851, Louis Napoleon staged a *coup d'état*—an army takeover of the government. Hugo had no choice but to flee the country. He escaped to Belgium in disguise, and eventually settled in Guernsey, a tiny island between England and France. From 1855 to 1870,

character, Hugo reversed the traditional identification of ugliness and deformity with evil.

Notre-Dame de Paris cast a spell over the French public, and made them more aware of their medieval past. It even inspired campaigns to preserve the nation's ancient monuments. And this tragic story still appeals to readers of all ages today.

Hugo lived there as an exile. When Louis Napoleon offered an amnesty to all political exiles—which meant that they were forgiven, and could go back to their homes—Hugo replied, "When freedom returns, I shall return!"

When Hugo arrived on Guernsey, he had little money, but his 1856 collection of poems, *Les Contemplations—The Meditations*—earned him enough to buy a mansion on the island. Then, in 1862, *Les Misérables—The Wretched*—was published. Widely seen as Hugo's finest novel, it follows the adventures of Jean Valjean, an ex-convict whose crime was to have stolen a loaf of bread. Through his hero's struggle to make a new life, Hugo shows the hardships faced daily by the poor. *Les Misérables* displays Hugo's love of high drama, but it also shows elements of Realism, a style that had become dominant in the French novel. Realist writers tried to reflect life as honestly as possible, rejecting the exaggerated dramatic effects of the Romantic novel.

A NATIONAL HERO

In 1870, Prussia—now part of Germany—invaded France, and Louis Napoleon's dictatorship fell. Hugo was welcomed back to France as a national hero who had stuck to his principles. His 80th birthday was celebrated as a national holiday. He continued to write great works right up until his death on May 18, 1885. His funeral was one of the great events of the century.

MAJOR WORKS

1822	ODES ET POÉSIES DIVERSES
1829	LES ORIENTALES
1830	HERNANI
1831	NOTRE-DAME DE PARIS
1856	LES CONTEMPLATIONS
1862	LES MISÉRABLES

Edgar Allan Poe

During his brief and unhappy life, Poe struggled against debt, depression, drink, and an obsession with death. His vivid imagination drove him to write haunting and macabre stories that still chill readers today.

Edgar Poe was born on January 19, 1809, in Boston, Massachusetts, the second child of two traveling actors, David and Elizabeth Poe. His father, who deserted the family soon after Edgar's birth, died of tuberculosis in 1810. A year later, his mother also died of the disease. Edgar, his brother Henry, and sister Rosalie, were left orphans.

A NEW FAMILY

Edgar went to live with John Allan, a wealthy Richmond merchant, and his wife Frances. The boy took his middle name from the family. He adored his foster mother, but his relationship with John was difficult. In 1815, the Allans moved to London, England. They returned to Richmond five years later.

Poe was a bright, sensitive boy. In 1826, he entered the University of Virginia in Charlottesville. His foster father gave him very little money, so Poe tried to win money by gambling. Depressed due to a failed romance, burdened with guilt, and with massive debts, he began drinking for the first time. After less than a year, Allan removed him from the university and took him back to Richmond. The relationship between Poe and Allan got worse.

Frances Allan, now herself ill with tuberculosis, tried to calm the situation. But in March 1827, after a quarrel with Allan, Poe left and went to Boston. There, he published a book of his poetry, *Tamerlane and other Poems*. It sold very badly. To save himself from poverty, he joined the army. He was a good soldier, rising to the rank of sergeant major in only 18 months.

In 1829, Poe received news that Frances was dying, and he got leave to be with her. But he was too late, arriving the day after her funeral. Grief-stricken, Poe obtained a discharge from the army. The next year, he entered the U.S. Military Academy at West Point.

Edgar Allan Poe, 1848, by S.W. Hawthorn **This photograph shows the sensitive and morbid writer a year before his sudden and mysterious death at the age of 40.**

The Masque of the Red Death, 1919, by Harry Clarke
In one of Poe's most memorable tales, knights and ladies enjoy a magnificent ball in Prince Prospero's castle, while outside, death stalks the land in the shape of a terrible plague, the Red Death. Suddenly, a terrifying, masked figure appears amid the revelers "shrouded… in the habiliments [dress] of the grave" and "dabbled in blood"—the Red Death itself.

But he neglected his duties, and was dismissed in January 1831.

He spent a month in New York, and had another book published. But he was still penniless. He went to Baltimore to live with his aunt, Maria Clemm, and her daughter, Virginia. They were just as poor as he was. Seeing a short story contest in a newspaper, Poe entered several works, including "Manuscript Found in a Bottle," which won the first prize.

The prize money was not enough to help the Clemm household, however. So Poe visited Allan, now on his death-bed, to ask for his help. As soon as the old man saw him, he began cursing. He died soon after, leaving Poe nothing.

A LITERARY CAREER

Poe was desperate to earn a living. In 1835, he returned to Richmond, and got a job on *The Southern Literary Messenger*. While working for the magazine, Poe won a reputation as a brilliant literary critic. But, lonely and depressed, he turned again to drink. His editor suspended him, saying: "No man is safe who drinks before breakfast."

When Poe heard that his cousin, Neilsen, had offered to take care of 13-year-old Virginia, he was distraught. On September 22, 1835, he went to Baltimore and secretly married her.

The marriage heralded a brief period of happiness for Poe. He was reinstated at the *Messenger*, and soon took over editorial control. Circulation soared and his reputation grew. But he was unhappy with the "contemptible" salary, and in 1837, he quit. He took his family to New York, and then to Philadelphia.

For the next five years, Poe worked on various publications. These printed some of his best-known stories, including "The Fall of the House of Usher" and "The Murders in the Rue Morgue," the world's first detective story.

Poe wrote in the Gothic tradition: His tales, such as "The Masque of the Red Death," dwell on the macabre and terrifying—death, disease, madness, murder, and the supernatural. His chilling horror stories evoke a nightmare world where evil always triumphs over good. During Poe's lifetime, many critics attacked the apparent lack of moral values in his works. Nonetheless, their dark beauty still inspires readers today.

TRAGEDY STRIKES AGAIN

Poe's happiness was short-lived. One evening in January 1842, Virginia coughed and blood ran down over her white dress. Poe immediately recognized the signs of tuberculosis. His despair drove him once more to the bottle.

Despite his heavy drinking, he wrote feverishly. In 1844, he moved back to New York. A year later, Poe's haunting poem "The Raven" was a great success. A typically atmospheric work, the poem made the writer internationally famous —but it did not make him any money.

Virginia's health worsened, and in 1847, she died. Overcome with grief, and often drunk, Poe lost his grip on sanity. Seeking comfort, he got engaged to a widow who was interested in literature. But she called the marriage off at the last minute. Poe returned to Richmond, where he met by chance a childhood friend, Elmira Shelton. She agreed to marry him—if he gave up drinking.

A MYSTERIOUS END

In September 1849, Poe stopped in Baltimore on his way to New York, and disappeared for five days. On October 3, a local doctor found him unconscious, dirty, and in borrowed clothes. He was rushed to the hospital, where he swung between consciousness and violent fits. For four days, he hovered on the brink of death. Then, in the early hours of October 7, 1849, he suddenly became quiet, whispered "Lord help my poor soul," and died. He was 40.

MAJOR WORKS

1840	THE FALL OF THE HOUSE OF USHER
1841	THE MURDERS IN THE RUE MORGUE
1842	THE MASQUE OF THE RED DEATH
1843	THE BLACK CAT
1845	THE RAVEN

THE BRONTËS

The three talented and imaginative Brontë sisters—Charlotte, Emily, and Anne—created extraordinary and deeply passionate works at a time when women's lives were restricted and difficult.

Charlotte Brontë, was born on April 21, 1816, in Thornton, in the north of England. She was the third daughter of the Reverend Patrick Brontë and his wife, Maria. The couple already had two daughters, Elizabeth and Maria. In 1817, the couple had a son, Branwell. The following year, Emily was born, on July 30, and Anne eighteen months later.

Soon after, the reverend was appointed to a new parish, and the family moved to the hill village of Haworth, amid the windswept Yorkshire moors of northern England. The bleak beauty of the landscape would have a strong influence on the children.

A DIFFICULT CHILDHOOD

A year after the family's move, Mrs. Brontë died of cancer. The children's aunt, Elizabeth Branwell, now brought them up. In 1824, Patrick Brontë found a school he could afford for his four eldest daughters, Charlotte, Maria, Elizabeth, and Emily. The girls were very unhappy there. The school did not

feed them properly, punished them continually, and generally neglected them. The conditions were so severe that in 1825, Maria and Elizabeth, the eldest Brontë sisters, died of tuberculosis. This deeply affected Charlotte, leaving her with a lasting bitterness. She and Emily were brought home.

LIFE AT HAWORTH

The four remaining children spent their childhood at Haworth in virtual isolation from the outside world. Patrick Brontë mostly stayed in his study—he even ate alone—and the children's aunt was cold and remote. The children had to entertain themselves.

Having no outsiders to play with, the young Brontës retreated into their own imaginary worlds. In 1826, not long after the girls had left their hated school, their father brought home a box of

Charlotte, Emily, and Anne Brontë (detail), 1840s, by Branwell Brontë
This portrait shows the three sisters in a typically reflective and somber mood.

wooden toy soldiers for Branwell. This was an exciting event in the children's lives. Each child chose a soldier, each with his own imaginary kingdom. They began writing stories based on the adventures of their adopted characters.

The wild Yorkshire countryside provided another welcome means of escape. Emily often disappeared on long walks of up to 20 miles a day across the moors. During her walks, her mind raced with the stories she had been told by Tabby, the housekeeper.

A NEW ROLE

Four years later, Patrick Brontë fell ill. This made him realize that his children did not have any training, and if he were to die, they would be poor. He therefore sent Charlotte to Miss Wooler's school at Roe Head. She was bright, and soon reached the top of her class. Within 18 months, she had absorbed all the school had to teach her and was back home.

In 1835, Roe Head offered Charlotte the post of assistant teacher. The salary was small, but it included free schooling for one of her sisters. Seizing the opportunity to help her family, she and Emily left Haworth again. Charlotte spent the next three years teaching. Then, between 1839 and 1841, she worked as a governess in private homes.

EMILY AND HAWORTH

Both Charlotte and Anne managed to hold jobs as governesses. But not Emily. She hated Roe Head so much that Charlotte feared for her life: "Liberty was the breath of Emily's nostrils, without it, she perished....

A WOMAN'S WORK

In the 19th century, a woman's "place" was the home. Yet women like the Brontës needed to work.

Like thousands of other women during the 19th century, the Brontë sisters faced a dilemma. They were too poor to live without working—yet they were ladies, and so could only do certain types of jobs. Almost all "ladylike" jobs were badly paid, exhausting, and humiliating.

There was little "suitable" work outside the home: Public office, the professions, and the universities were all closed to women. Some gentlewomen worked as seamstresses. Other possibilities included working as a teacher, or—like Charlotte Brontë and her heroine, Jane Eyre—a governess (*above right*).

Every morning when she woke, the vision of home and the moors rushed on her ... her health was quickly broken.... I felt in my heart she would die if she did not go home...."

After just three months, Emily returned to Haworth. There, she spent nearly all her time with Branwell, who had ambitions as an artist and writer. She felt herself a failure and withdrew

The work was virtually slave labor. A governess often worked for long hours and little pay. And her position was often lonely— as a lady she could not mix with the servants, and yet she could socialize with her employers only when invited.

Marriage was the other way of escaping poverty. Yet this brought severe restrictions to an independent-minded woman: Women had to submit to their husband's will at all times.

from the world. She took comfort from her pets, which included pigeons and geese. She also taught herself German, played the piano, and wrote poetry. In 1837, she tried again to live in the outside world, and took a job as a governess. But she was desperately unhappy, and returned once more to Haworth.

Both Charlotte and Anne, meanwhile, felt lonely and isolated living away from home. So they decided to open their own school, with money from their aunt. First, to perfect their French and improve their German, Charlotte and Emily went to a school in Brussels, Belgium, in 1842.

Emily left no record of her experiences in Belgium. But the trip had a strong impact on Charlotte's life. She fell passionately in love with Constantin Héger, husband of the school's principal. The sisters returned to Haworth when their aunt died in November, but Charlotte soon went back to Brussels as a teacher. She was lonely there. Her greatest joy was giving Monsieur Héger English lessons.

WRITING IN EARNEST

After a year, Charlotte left Brussels, her unrequited passion still intense. In Haworth, she found that her father was nearly blind, and realized that she had to dedicate herself to nursing him, rather than to the planned school. She wrote passionate letters to Héger, but received no reply. Her misery prompted her to start writing, something she had barely done since 1839. She also composed a great deal of poetry.

From 1843, Branwell worked away from home as a tutor. He returned home in 1845. He had wasted his early artistic promise, and he now drank heavily. He became addicted to opium—a drug— spending his days either barely conscious, or delirious.

In late 1845, Charlotte discovered two scruffy notebooks containing poems written by Emily. She was instantly impressed by their extraordinary

Haworth Parsonage, Yorkshire, England
The Brontë family moved to this dark and austere parsonage when Charlotte was four. It would be their lifelong home. The house and its setting—a steep hill-village surrounded by the bleak beauty of the Yorkshire moors—was a vital influence on the Brontë children.

quality. Emily was furious with her sister for reading them, accusing Charlotte of betrayal. With Anne's help, however, Charlotte managed to persuade Emily that the three of them should contribute some of their poems to a joint volume of verse.

The sisters published the volume in 1846, under the names Currer, Ellis, and Acton Bell—chosen to correspond to their initials. The names meant that nobody could tell if the authors were male or female: It was rare for women to write books at the time. The book failed, but all three sisters were now writing regularly.

In July 1847, Emily's only novel was published. *Wuthering Heights* was a passionate and unconventional love story set against the desolate Yorkshire moors. It is the tragic, yet epic, story of Heathcliff and Catherine, who are kept apart by society. The intense passion between the two is echoed in the wild moors and violent weather. When Catherine dies, Heathcliff is haunted, and sets out to destroy and torment the next generation of their families.

Emily's courage and refusal to compromise resulted in one of the century's most passionate and controversial books. The critics of the time condemned the book as "disgusting," "evil," and "artistically immature." Emily ignored such reactions. After her death, it became recognized as a masterpiece.

JANE EYRE

The same year, Charlotte wrote *Jane Eyre*, a novel exploring a woman's right to retain her independent spirit. The story tells of Jane, an orphan, who—like Charlotte Brontë herself—works as a governess. She falls in love with her employer, Edward Rochester. But on their wedding day, she discovers that he is already married—to a woman who is insane, and kept locked in the attic of Rochester's home.

The novel traces a woman's struggle to establish her own identity, and highlights the injustice of Victorian attitudes to women. The book's originality and emotional power met with a glowing reception. Meanwhile, Anne wrote two novels, *Agnes Grey* and *The Tenant of Wildfell Hall* of 1847 and 1848, which also discussed women's place in society.

Tragedy was soon to shatter the Brontë family. Within a year of the publication of *Wuthering Heights*, Branwell was dead, destroyed by tuberculosis, alcohol, and drugs. At his funeral, in October 1848, Emily caught a cold; two months later, she died. By the following spring, Anne had also died of tuberculosis.

CHARLOTTE'S LAST YEARS

Charlotte now began a strange double life. As her reputation as a novelist grew, she had to combine taking care of her father at home with mixing in glittering literary social circles.

Soon after Charlotte completed *Villette*, in 1852, Patrick Brontë's curate, Arthur Bell Nicholls, asked her to marry him. Her father did not approve of the match, however, and the couple did not marry for a year and a half. Even then, Patrick Brontë refused to attend the wedding; the only guest was Charlotte's friend, Ellen Nussey.

The couple set up home in Haworth. Soon afterward, Charlotte became pregnant. But she was too frail, and died on March 31, 1855. The first novel she had written, *The Professor*, was published two years later.

MAJOR WORKS

1846	POEMS
1847	WUTHERING HEIGHTS; JANE EYRE; AGNES GREY
1848	THE TENANT OF WILDFELL HALL
1852	VILLETTE
1857	THE PROFESSOR

LUDWIG VAN BEETHOVEN

Although he was totally deaf for the last ten years of his life, Beethoven produced some of the finest music the world has ever heard. Today, his work is performed more than that of any other composer.

Ludwig van Beethoven was born on December 17, 1770, in Bonn, a city in western Germany. He came from a musical family. His grandfather had been the musical director at the chapel of the elector, or prince, of Cologne. Beethoven's father, Johann, was also a musician, and taught his son to play the piano and violin at an early age.

The boy showed great talent, and by the age of 13, he was playing in the elector's orchestra. At 14, he was appointed assistant chapel organist. Beethoven's home life was not so happy. His father drank too much, and was cruel to Maria, Beethoven's mother.

The elector had a high opinion of Beethoven, and in 1787, he sent the young man to Vienna, the capital of Austria and an important musical center. There Beethoven played before the great composer Mozart, who remarked, "Watch this lad.... Someday he will force the world to talk about him."

Beethoven returned to Bonn when he heard that his mother was very ill. Both she and Beethoven's baby sister died in 1787. By the time Johann died in 1792, Beethoven was the family's main breadwinner.

RETURN TO VIENNA

In November 1792, Beethoven returned to Vienna to study with the famous composer Joseph Haydn. The partnership was not very successful. Beethoven, now aged 22, was a little too old to make a good pupil, and Haydn was too busy to devote time to him anyway. Beethoven later claimed that he had "never learned anything from Haydn."

Despite this, Beethoven soon made a name for himself as a very talented pianist. Rejecting the restrained classical style of playing, Beethoven performed with such power that he had to ask piano manufacturers to build stronger, louder models.

Ludwig van Beethoven, 1818,
by Ferdinand Schimon
Shown here in his late forties, Beethoven was famous for his wild appearance.

Before long, Beethoven had found a patron in Prince Karl Lichnowsky. The prince and his wife invited him to move into their apartments and paid him a generous allowance. This gave Beethoven the freedom to concentrate on composing. In return, he dedicated his first major works to Lichnowsky.

Beethoven was a proud man, however, and was uncomfortable with patronage. He held the Romantic belief that great artists were more important than noblemen, and should be treated with the utmost respect. After one argument with Lichnowsky, Beethoven wrote angrily to his patron, "There have been thousands of princes. There is only one Beethoven."

A TRAGIC LOSS

As Beethoven was charming Vienna with his music, a terrible thing was happening—he was slowly going deaf. He finally admitted it to himself in 1801, at the age of 31, although he had known it in his heart for some time. "I shall be the unhappiest of God's creatures," he wrote to a friend. "I live only in music." For the last ten years of his life he would be totally deaf.

Deafness put an end to his career as a pianist, and made it difficult for him to conduct his own works. He became moody and eccentric, cutting himself off from the world and neglecting his appearance. His rooms were a mess of manuscripts, musical instruments, and the remains of meals.

In 1802, Beethoven's doctor advised him to escape from his busy life in Vienna for a while. For six months, he

THE SYMPHONY

Beethoven developed the structure of the symphony and enriched it with emotional expressiveness.

The modern symphony is an orchestral piece which developed in the 18th century from the overture—the orchestral part of an opera or a play. It is usually arranged into fast and slow parts, called movements.

The first great masters of the symphony were Mozart and Haydn. In their hands, it became the most profound form of music that a composer could write. They composed in the classical style: Their work was balanced and structured, and aimed at pure musical beauty rather than at the expression of emotion.

Beethoven composed his first two symphonies in this style. But

stayed in the nearby village of Heiligenstadt, coming to terms with his deafness. He considered suicide, but decided eventually to return to Vienna and dedicate his life to his work.

A NEW STYLE

Most of Beethoven's early works belonged to the classical tradition of his teacher Haydn. But piano sonatas like his third, *Eroica*, was very different. Widely seen as the first Romantic symphony, it is longer, bolder, and more emotionally intense than either Mozart's or Haydn's symphonies.

Today, Beethoven's nine symphonies are performed more often than those of any other composer. The opening bar of the best known of these, Symphony No. 5 (*above*)—three short notes followed by a longer, lower one—is one of the most famous musical phrases ever written. Symphony No. 9, which Beethoven wrote when he was completely deaf, is seen by many as his finest work.

the *Pathétique* and the *Moonlight*—both of which Beethoven had written before he realized that he was going deaf—suggested that he was moving away from the orderly, structured approach of Classicism toward the freedom and passion of Romanticism.

On his return from Heiligenstadt, Beethoven decided to change direction completely. "I am only a little satisfied with my previous works," he wrote. "From now on I will take a new path." Between 1803 and 1824, Beethoven wrote seven symphonies—numbers three to nine. These works mark the transition to the Romantic era in music.

As Beethoven composed his greatest works, he enjoyed increased financial security. When he received an offer of employment from a court in Germany, three Austrian noblemen awarded him a generous annual salary in order to keep him in Vienna. One of the noblemen, the Archduke Rudolf, remained a friend and patron for the rest of the composer's life.

In 1815, Beethoven's brother Caspar died. The composer took on the responsibility of looking after Caspar's son, Karl. Although much of Beethoven's time was now taken up by his nephew, he wrote some of his greatest masterpieces, including Symphony No. 9 and the *Missa Solemnis*. Beethoven died in Vienna on March 26, 1827. The whole city mourned his death, and 10,000 people followed the funeral procession.

MAJOR WORKS

1799	PATHÉTIQUE
1800-01	MOONLIGHT SONATA
1803-04	SYMPHONY NO. 3 (EROICA)
1807-08	SYMPHONY NO. 5
1817-23	SYMPHONY NO. 9
1819-23	MISSA SOLEMNIS

FRANZ SCHUBERT

Schubert's life was brief and unhappy, but immensely creative. Much of his work was not performed in his lifetime, but his symphonies and *lieds*—poems set to music—display a wonderful melodic gift.

Franz Schubert was born in Vienna, Austria, on January 31, 1797, the 12th of 14 children. His father ran a school in the family house. Schubert attended his father's school, and showed great musical ability from an early age.

In 1808, the 11-year-old Schubert joined the boys' choir at the Imperial and Royal Seminary—the best music college in Vienna. Although he was shy and often homesick, he was an outstanding student. In 1813, just before Schubert left, his First Symphony was performed by the seminary orchestra.

A TEENAGE MAESTRO

In 1814, at the age of just 17, Schubert became a music teacher at his father's school, where he stayed until 1818. During these four years, he composed over 400 works, including five symphonies. At the time, Vienna was dominated by the influence of Beethoven (*see page 64*), and the legacy of Wolfgang Amadeus Mozart, who had died six years before Schubert's birth.

The young composer's early symphonies were influenced by the work of these two men. Meanwhile, in his *lieds*—which means "songs" in German—he was developing his own, unique style.

MASTER OF THE SONG

Schubert was the first of the great composers to concentrate on the *lied*. In the course of his life, he wrote more than 600. Schubert lived in a golden age of German poetry. He had a great love of literature, and many of his songs were settings of poems. His sensitivity to literature helped him blend words and music closely. An example of this is his *Gretchen at the Spinning Wheel* (1814), which he set to *Faust*, a play by Germany's leading Romantic writer, Goethe. The piano accompaniment to the melody suggests the monotonous movement of the spinning wheel itself.

Franz Schubert, 1827, by Franz Eybl
This painting shows Schubert in the year before he died. He was at the height of his powers as a composer at this time.

A Schubert evening in a Vienna town house, 1897, by Julius Schmid
This painting recreates the atmosphere of one of the "Schubertiads"—evenings organized by Schubert's friends and dedicated to the performance of his works.

Schubert's gift for melody came surprisingly easily. He was able to compose at breakneck speed. Amazed friends reported that he would read a poem through a couple of times, and then write down the music as quickly as if he were writing a letter. He did not use a piano, claiming that it made him lose his train of thought. In just one year, 1815, he composed around 145 songs.

BREAKING AWAY

Schubert did not enjoy teaching, and in 1818, he left home to pursue a career as a composer. He would never make much money, and little of his work would be published in his lifetime. One reason for this was that, unlike most of the leading composers of his time, he was not an outstanding musician, and could not promote his own work by performing it in public.

Yet money was not very important to Schubert. He lived a carefree life, spending much of his time in coffeehouses with his friends, who were all musicians, artists, and writers. Schubert wrote most of his works simply for his friends to perform and enjoy.

Schubert's friends helped to made his work popular by sponsoring and organizing "Schubertiads." These were musical evenings in which nothing but Schubert's work was performed. Whereas Beethoven and Mozart had spent much of their time in the courts of kings and aristocrats, "Schubertiads" took place privately in modest middle-class homes. Meanwhile, one of Schubert's friends, the opera singer Johann Vogl, helped by performing his songs in public. Schubert's reputation grew, and in 1822, one critic called him "a genius."

That same year, Schubert became very sick. The rest of his life would be

> "He bade poetry sound and music speak."
> (Austrian poet, Franz Grillparzer)

dogged by illness. "There is no man in the world as wretched and unhappy as I," he wrote. It was a bleak time. That year he wrote his Eighth Symphony—the *Unfinished*. It has a dark quality that reflects the depth of his suffering. Yet it was far more confident than his earlier symphonies, and displayed the loose, melodic beauty of his song-writing. Only the first two movements survive—what happened to the final two remains a mystery.

LAST YEARS

Despite continued ill health and bouts of depression, Schubert's powers as a composer continued to grow. In 1827, he wrote a collection of songs, *Winter Journey*, based on a set of poems by Wilhelm Müller, a German poet. They tell the story of a sad musician, playing

on the street in winter. Nobody gives him any money or listens to his music. It is likely that Schubert saw similarities between himself and the miserable musician. *Winter Journey* made even his most cheerful friends feel gloomy.

Yet however disappointed Schubert was with his life at this time, he also managed to produce uplifting, beautiful music such as the *Death and the Maiden* quartet (1824). His reputation continued to grow slowly, and March 1828 saw a public concert of his music.

In the same year, Schubert finished his Ninth Symphony—known as *The Great*. The orchestra for which it was intended found it too difficult to play, however, and it was not performed during his lifetime. The huge work was rediscovered a decade after Schubert's death. Many place it alongside Beethoven's Ninth as one of the greatest symphonies ever composed.

This symphony was Schubert's last work. The composer fell ill in 1828. He was still able to work and go for walks until November 11, when he took to his bed. He died on November 19, 1828.

MAJOR WORKS

1814	GRETCHEN AT THE SPINNING WHEEL
1822	SYMPHONY NO. 8 (THE UNFINISHED)
1824	DEATH AND THE MAIDEN
1827	WINTER JOURNEY
1828	SYMPHONY NO. 9 (THE GREAT)

HECTOR BERLIOZ

Throughout his uneasy life, Berlioz was celebrated as a genius by some, and labeled an untalented eccentric by others. Now, however, he is recognized as one of the most original Romantic composers.

Hector Berlioz was born on December 11, 1803, at La Côte-St. André, southeast France. As a boy, he learned to play the flute, guitar, and recorder, and by his early teens, he had composed his first pieces. But his father, the local doctor, wanted him to have a career in medicine. In 1821, he sent Hector to a medical school in Paris.

The 18-year-old Berlioz was soon bored with his medical studies, and he turned toward music instead. He attended performances at the Opéra, and tried to improve his own technique by copying out other composers' scores.

THE TRUE VOCATION

Berlioz's neglect of his studies made his parents very angry, and they threatened to cut off his allowance. But their son passionately defended his decision to follow a musical career. In the end, his parents made a deal with him: He would study music for a trial period on the understanding that, if he failed, he would return to medicine.

But he was determined to succeed. In 1826, he enrolled at the Paris music school, the Conservatory. That year, he entered the school's Prix de Rome. The prize for the winner of this prestigious competition was a period of study in Rome. The judges, however, declared the work Berlioz entered "unplayable."

INFATUATION

In 1827, while watching a play, Berlioz became infatuated with one of the actresses, Harriet Smithson. For two years, he bombarded her with adoring letters, until she finally refused to accept any more. Distraught, Berlioz poured his feelings into his *Symphonie Fantastique*—a musical representation of his unrequited passions. The first performance of the work in December 1830 was a great success. At the end, the audience cheered and clapped

Hector Berlioz, 1832, by Émile Signol
As a young man, Berlioz was famous for his strange appearance. A friend described the composer's hair as "an immense umbrella."

loudly, and demanded an encore. Reviews the next day were full of praise.

Encouraged by this reaction, Berlioz entered more works for the Prix de Rome. In 1830, at his fourth attempt, the judges voted him the winner. The following year, he left for Rome, where he stayed for the next 12 months.

Back in Paris in 1832, Berlioz finally met Harriet Smithson and the couple began a stormy affair. On one occasion, when Harriet accused Berlioz of not loving her, he took poison in front of her. They married on October 3, 1833, and had a son, Louis, ten months later.

BATTLE FOR ACCEPTANCE

Berlioz described the period from then until his retirement as "my 30 years' war against the deaf." His music had become so original that most people could not understand it, and many hated it. It broke the accepted rules of harmony and used a new type of melody.

In 1838, *Benvenuto Cellini*, an opera he had completed the year before, failed miserably. The cost of its production plunged Berlioz into debt. To earn some money, he wrote music criticism. His articles were highly provocative and showed how much he disagreed with the musical standards of the day.

Throughout his 30s, he wrote several new compositions, each time shocking the audience with his bizarre music and outrageous behavior. At one open-air performance of his *Grand Funeral and Triumphal Symphony*, he conducted a full orchestra and brass band of 200 performers with a drawn sword. At the end, he collapsed across the kettle-

SYMPHONIE FANTASTIQUE

Unrequited love, passion, and death are some of the ingredients of Berlioz's most original and inventive work.

Berlioz's *Symphonie Fantastique* is often seen as the first example of Romantic program music, or music that tells a story. Berlioz wrote the work as a way of describing his heartbreak at being rejected by Harriet Smithson.

He took the innovative step of handing out a program to the audience so that they could understand the feelings described by the music. He did not identify the characters, but it was easy for the audience to recognize them as Berlioz and Harriet.

The symphony recounts the pair's stormy love affair. Passion, rejection, and murder are the major themes. It was unusual for

drums, weeping. Such an unconventional style earned Berlioz many enemies within the French musical establishment, and won him a reputation among the public as an eccentric.

In 1841, Berlioz's marriage to Harriet ended, and he began a liaison with Marie Recio, a singer. Despite his lack of success in France, recognition was more forthcoming elsewhere in Europe.

an orchestral work to deal with such subjects. The piece was also original in playing contrasting instruments, such as horns and violins, against each other so that they seem to argue. The effect was so unsettling that one critic wrote that Berlioz "invents new rhythm."

The composer's odd style of performance made him an easy target, both for critics, and for cartoonists (*above*). Yet when he first performed the *Symphonie* in December 1830, the reception was ecstatic.

During the 1840s and 1850s, he toured widely, visiting England, Russia, and Germany. Everywhere, audiences and critics alike acclaimed him as a genius.

In 1854, Harriet died. Despite their separation, Berlioz grieved deeply. He married Marie shortly after. The marriage coincided with a time of growing despair for Berlioz. He had still not achieved recognition in France. In

1858, he completed an opera, *Les Troyens*, or *The Trojans*, a colossal piece based on the ancient Roman epic poem, the *Aeneid*. Berlioz considered the work to be his greatest. But it was too long to be staged in one performance, and Berlioz had to cut it down into two, much shorter operas. In the end, only one of these was performed. This upset the composer immensely.

OLD AGE AND DECLINE

The final years of his life were a depressing time for Berlioz. He suffered from an acute intestinal disorder, which gave him constant pain, and in 1862, Marie died. In his grief, he resolved to stop composing. The death of his son, Louis, in 1867 was a further blow. Berlioz's only pleasure after this was a year-long conducting trip to Russia.

He returned from Russia in 1868, exhausted and depressed. He died on March 8, 1869, at the age of 66. Just before his death, Berlioz proclaimed that his life had been a mistake and his genius an illusion. Yet the rich passion and imagination that so shocked his contemporaries continue to inspire generations of new composers.

MAJOR WORKS	
1830	SYMPHONIE FANTASTIQUE
1837	BENVENUTO CELLINI
1840	GRAND FUNERAL AND TRIUMPHAL SYMPHONY
1858	LES TROYENS

FRÉDÉRIC CHOPIN

Before his early death at the age of 39, Chopin dazzled audiences with his remarkable piano skills and intensely personal compositions. His unique style dominated piano music throughout the 19th century.

Frédéric François Chopin was born on March 1, 1810, just outside the Polish capital, Warsaw. His father, Nicolas, had left his native France as a youth and settled in Poland, where he met and married Justina Krzyzanowska.

Chopin was a precocious child. He drew cartoons, wrote plays and verses, and—without any training—composed and played his own piano pieces. In 1817, when he was only seven, he had his first composition published. His fame spread quickly, and at the age of eight, he gave his first public concert.

In 1826, he enrolled at Warsaw's music school, the Conservatory. Warsaw, however, was something of a musical backwater. Before long, Chopin felt the need to go abroad in search of more enriching musical experiences.

In 1829, he traveled to Austria. That August, he made his professional debut in Vienna, a far more musically sophisticated city than Warsaw. He played several concerts and got a tremendous reception. His youthful brilliance startled the Viennese. Fired by this success, he returned to Warsaw, more determined than ever to make his name outside his native country.

On November 2, 1830, Chopin left Poland for good, although the spirit of his homeland would affect his work throughout his life. The influence of traditional Polish folk music gave all his works a pervasive sense of melancholy.

SUCCESS IN PARIS

In 1831, after a few months back in Vienna, Chopin settled in Paris. Before long, he was short of money. He managed to support himself by teaching the piano to fellow Poles in the city. His fortunes changed, however, after he gave a stunning performance at the home of the wealthy Rothschild family. At once, Chopin became the most sought-after piano teacher in Paris. He

Frédéric Chopin, 1838,
by Eugène Delacroix
The famous French Romantic artist shows his composer friend at the age of 28.

76

could now charge large sums for lessons, and could afford to live in luxury.

Meanwhile, he was composing steadily—mainly solo piano pieces. His works extended piano technique as it was then known. Chopin's fingering of the keys, use of pedals, and new rhythms increased the piano's range of sounds. His style would dominate piano music for the rest of the century.

Chopin's concert career, however, was not so successful. He had neither the physical stamina nor the temperament for the demanding life of a concert pianist. His playing style was quiet, and therefore not suited to large concert halls, and he had stage fright before each performance.

LOVE AND SICKNESS
In Paris, Chopin became part of the circle of Romantic artists, writers, and musicians. These included the Hungarian composer Franz Liszt (*see page 80*). Through Liszt, Chopin met the French novelist George Sand. Sand was fascinated by genius; she had had affairs with several of the Romantics, including the artist, Eugène Delacroix (*see page 28*). In the summer of 1838, Chopin and Sand began a relationship.

The couple spent that winter on the Mediterranean island of Majorca. For a number of years, Chopin had been suffering from tuberculosis. The warm climate eased his pain, but as the weather became damper and windier, the illness worsened.

In February 1839, Chopin and Sand returned to France, and their life fell into a regular pattern. They spent the

CHOPIN'S PIANO MUSIC

More than any other composer, Chopin has become associated with one instrument—the piano.

Chopin spent most of his career composing for the piano. In his day, the instrument was still fairly new and uncommon. Chopin showed the piano's potential, and helped establish it as one of the most popular instruments. In recognition of this, in 1848, an English piano company presented their most expensive model (*above right*) to the composer.

Chopin produced piano music of varying weight and complexity. On one hand, he wrote light pieces, known as "salon" pieces, after the elegant private rooms in which they were played. On another, he created full-scale concert works of great emotion.

summers at Sand's country retreat, and the winters in Paris. During the years he lived with Sand, Chopin wrote some of his best works. When he was not giving lessons or composing, Chopin spent much of his time with Sand's two children, whom he adored.

Chopin's health worsened, however. Nonetheless, he decided to yield to his friends' requests, and give a public

Some of his music requires breathtaking skill from the pianist. A contemporary musician described Chopin's pieces as "unplayable, finger-breaking exercises," and a critic advised pianists to have a doctor nearby before attempting them.

When he performed his own music, Chopin never played the same piece twice in the same way. He altered the speed, volume, and even occasionally the notes themselves. This made it seem as if he were making up the music on the spot. In fact, he had composed it very slowly and carefully.

performance. The prospect brought on a nightmare of doubts and stress. His fears were misplaced, however. The concert, in April 1841, was a dazzling event. It received excellent reviews and raised a huge sum of money.

The composer's precarious health was not helped by an increasingly difficult domestic situation, as his relationship with George Sand broke down.

In 1847, after bitter arguments, the relationship finally ended.

Chopin's spirits plummeted, and he gave up all interest in composition. To take his mind off things, his friends again persuaded him to give a public concert. A former pupil, Jane Stirling, supported him during his customary preconcert nervous agonies.

THE FINAL YEARS

In April 1848, Chopin and Stirling traveled to Britain. Although desperately ill, he gave several concerts. He found Stirling—who wanted to marry him—irritating. Using the English climate as an excuse, he returned home.

A brief improvement in his condition gave Chopin a few happy months. Some of the inspiration that had deserted him on his break with Sand returned, and he produced two mazurkas—traditional Polish dances—for the piano.

Then he had a relapse. With his sister, Ludwika, by his side, Chopin died in Paris on October 17, 1849. He was just 39 years old. After his burial, Ludwika took his heart back to Poland, in accordance with his last request.

MAJOR WORKS

1829-32	12 ÉTUDES: OPUS 10
1830	PIANO CONCERTO NO. 1 IN E MINOR
1836-39	24 PRELUDES
1837	FUNERAL MARCH
1842	BALLADE IN F MINOR

FRANZ LISZT

As a brilliant pianist, passionate lover, man of religion, and composer of genius, Franz Liszt embodied the ambitions, achievements, and contradictions of the Romantic movement.

Franz Liszt was born on October 22, 1811 in the village of Raiding, Hungary. His father, Adam, who could play most instruments, taught him to play the piano. The boy made remarkable progress, and he gave his first concert when he was just nine years old.

In 1820, the family moved to the Austrian capital, Vienna. There Liszt studied with a leading pianist, Carl Czerny, who said, "I never had such a diligent, gifted, and ardent pupil." When he was 11 years old, Liszt had his first composition published.

A CHILD STAR

In Vienna, Liszt gave several concerts. Legend has it that after one, the elderly Ludwig van Beethoven (*see page 64*), climbed onto the stage to kiss the boy. Such success convinced Adam Liszt that his son should tour Europe. After returning to their native Hungary, the family left for Germany and then Paris.

As a foreigner, Liszt could not enter the famous Paris music school, the Conservatory. While in Paris, he met a noted piano manufacturer, Sebastian Erard, who had invented a new kind of piano which allowed the player to repeat notes very rapidly. Wanting to publicize his product, Erard supplied the boy with a piano for his tour.

The family moved to London, where Liszt again enjoyed great success. But in 1827, Adam Liszt died of typhoid in France, where the family had gone to rest after their exhausting travels. His father's death left Liszt disillusioned with the life of a traveling prodigy. He felt that his art was little more than "amusement for fashionable society."

But he had to make a living. He settled in Paris with his mother and gave lessons to the daughters of the fashionable and wealthy. During his time in Paris, Liszt met the composers Hector Berlioz and Frédéric Chopin

Franz Liszt
The elderly composer and virtuoso pianist poses at his piano for this rather formal, undated photograph.

(*see pages 72 and 76*). He also heard the virtuoso violinist, Nicolò Paganini, play. Paganini's skill threw Liszt into a frenzy. He wanted to capture the same passionate brilliance on the piano.

Early in 1833, Liszt began an affair with Marie d'Agoult, a rich and well-educated countess. Although the relationship lasted for more than a decade—during which time the couple had three children—Liszt became bored with Marie after only a couple of years.

ON THE ROAD AGAIN

In 1837, Liszt began a period of intensive travel and concerts. Everywhere he went, he received the highest accolades, and his performances were greeted with enthusiastic adulation. One contemporary dubbed this mass hysteria "Lisztomania." Women adored Liszt's romantic looks as much as his brilliant playing, and the composer had several affairs during these years of nonstop travel. By 1844, Marie had had enough, and she ended the relationship.

Liszt's last journey of this period was a concert tour of Russia, where he met Princess Carolyne Sayn-Wittgenstein. He stayed on her estate for several days before giving his final public concert. At only 35, Liszt was weary of constantly performing. He was now ready to settle down to composing.

In 1848, Liszt took up a post as music director in the German town of Weimar. He set to work composing an astonishing amount of music: 12 symphonic poems, seven concertos, two symphonies, a large number of choral works, and many other piano pieces. He

THE GREAT VIRTUOSOS

With their breathtaking technical brilliance, virtuoso musicians became the superstars of the age.

Until the 19th century, the musician had been little more than a servant to high society. His playing was mere background music to the audience's conversations. But the arrival of several larger-than-life personalities, such as Liszt and the violinist Nicolò Paganini, changed the musician's status forever.

These performers were not just accomplished musicians, they were also great showmen. People began to go to concerts not simply for the music, but also to be enthralled and amazed by the agility of the performers. When Liszt stormed up and down the keyboard (*above right*),

also taught the piano, and conducted works by young composers, such as Richard Wagner, who later married one of Liszt's daughters, Cosima.

In 1860, Liszt and Carolyne traveled to Rome, where they intended to marry. The wedding was canceled at the last moment, however, when the pope refused to grant Carolyne a divorce from her first husband. The couple

In Rome, Liszt composed mainly religious music. One of the works of this period was the *Hungarian Coronation Mass*, written to mark the coronation of Franz Josef I as king of Hungary. When Liszt left the church after the ceremony, his fellow Hungarians cheered so loudly that people assumed he was the king himself.

CONTINUED ORIGINALITY

Gradually, Liszt emerged from his retreat. From around 1869, he spent the rest of his life traveling between Weimar, Budapest, and Rome. His compositions were now shorter and simpler, and more religious in feeling. He was striving toward daring new means of musical expression; many of these pieces were so original that they were never performed in his lifetime.

the audience became hysterical. Paganini played at breakneck speed, sometimes at 12 notes per second. He had a hypnotic effect; people said they could see the devil standing at his elbow. And Liszt's great rival, Sigismond Thalberg, had a technique so fantastic it was rumored that he had three hands.

The virtuosos had an exhausting life. They tried to outdo each other with the flamboyance of their performances, and went on long, demanding tours. Paganini, for example, played 112 shows in less than a year from spring 1831 to 1832.

As ever, women found him irresistible, and his last entanglement was with a pupil, Olga Janina. She became infatuated with Liszt, and took poison when he refused her advances.

In 1886, Liszt went to Bayreuth, Germany, to visit Cosima. On the way, he caught a cold, which developed into pneumonia. On July 31, 1886, he died.

separated. Two years later, Liszt's daughter, Blandine, died in childbirth. In his grief, the composer turned toward religion. He decided to enter the Catholic Church, and became an abbé. Liszt stayed in Rome for the rest of the decade, and gradually withdrew from public life. Friends noted that he was aging rapidly and was constantly worried about his health.

MAJOR WORKS

1851-4	HUNGARIAN RHAPSODIES: NOS. 1 TO 15
1854-57	FAUST SYMPHONY
1856	DANTE SYMPHONY
1867	HUNGARIAN CORONATION MASS

PETER ILYICH TCHAIKOVSKY

Probably the most popular of all Russian composers, Tchaikovsky had a remarkable gift for melody. He expressed his passions in music, creating works that were emotionally charged and deeply felt.

Peter Ilyich Tchaikovsky was born on May 7, 1840, at Votkinsk in Russia. From an early age, he showed great musical talent. He also had a very sensitive nature: After one musical evening, the boy sat up in bed crying, "This music! This music! It's here in my head and won't let me sleep."

Tchaikovsky was devastated when his mother died in 1854. He found his comfort in music—both in piano and singing lessons, and in his first attempts at composition.

In 1859, Tchaikovsky graduated from law school, and began work as a law clerk. The work bored him, and he concentrated on studying harmony and composition at the Russian Musical Society, which later became the St. Petersburg Conservatory. In 1863, he enrolled there as a full-time music student.

Tchaikovsky studied with Anton Rubinstein, the conservatory's director. Rubinstein's pianist brother, Nikolay, offered Tchaikovsky a post as teacher of harmony at the Moscow Conservatory. In 1866, Tchaikovsky moved to Moscow and joined Rubinstein's household. He wrote his first masterpiece, the concert overture, *Romeo and Juliet*, four years later.

A DIFFICULT TIME

Tchaikovsky enjoyed Moscow's lively cultural life, but he found the constant stream of visitors to Rubinstein's house tiring. In 1871, he left and moved into a small apartment of his own.

It was a difficult time for the composer. He was musically successful, but very lonely. His loneliness was worsened by bouts of severe depression, and hallucinations. Eventually, he suffered a nervous collapse. His doctor declared him "one step away from insanity."

Despite his troubles, Tchaikovsky was becoming a successful composer. In 1871, his First String Quartet was well received. During the decade, he

Peter Ilyich Tchaikovsky
This undated, formal photograph shows the composer when he was about 50 years old.

showed how versatile he was. He completed string quartets and an opera. In 1875, he began work on his Third Symphony, and on a ballet, *Swan Lake*. His one weakness was a fear of performing.

The same year saw the premiere of the First Piano Concerto, which to many represents the pinnacle of Romantic piano music. Yet at the time, many people criticized it. After the work's first performance, in Boston in October 1875, one critic asked, "Could we ever learn to love such music?" The work was exciting—yet it was also difficult, strange, and wild.

NEW RELATIONSHIPS

As he approached his late thirties, two women changed the composer's life. The first was a wealthy widow, Nadezdha von Meck, who commissioned a piece from him. She and Tchaikovsky became friends, and in 1876, they began writing to each other. She wrote to him that "… your music makes my life easier and more pleasant to live."

Tchaikovsky's new patron gave him a generous allowance, and also offered emotional support. They shared many secrets, but never met. Their friendship revolved around music. The widow described how his melodies would bring on breathlessness, weeping, even fainting.

In May 1877, Tchaikovsky received a letter from one of his students, Antonina Milyukova. She threatened to kill herself if he refused to meet her. She was obsessed. Tchaikovsky felt trapped: "Either I must keep my freedom at the expense of this woman's ruin … or I must marry." Less than a month after

MUSIC FOR BALLET

Ballet music offered Tchaikovsky an escape from the fears and frustrations of the outside world.

Although other composers regarded ballet music as second-rate, Tchaikovsky felt it deserved as much attention as opera. "I cannot understand why the term should be … disapproving," he declared. "There is such a thing as good ballet music."

During Tchaikovsky's lifetime, Russia dominated the world of ballet. The composer's first full-length ballet was *Swan Lake*, a story of a swan princess (*above right*), half mortal and half immortal. It was only a moderate success. Eleven years later, in 1888, Tchaikovsky started work on *The Sleeping Beauty*, which was much more successful.

their first meeting, he proposed to her; they were married soon after.

The marriage was a disaster. After they returned from their honeymoon, Tchaikovsky tried to commit suicide and suffered a mental breakdown. The couple separated, and later divorced.

Once he had recovered, Tchaikovsky threw himself into composing. He worked obsessively on his Fourth Sym-

Following the ballet's favorable reception, Tchaikovsky wrote *The Nutcracker* in 1891. The ballet tells of children's toys coming to life. It captured the imagination of the audience. This work offered Tchaikovsky the chance to give full rein to his imagination, particularly in his use of instrumentation and varied dance rhythms. All three scores remain favorites today.

phony, a work that expressed his emotional turmoil. And in 1878, he finished his greatest opera, *Eugene Onegin*. But he was restless, and traveled constantly. Of the *1812 Overture* of 1880, one of his most popular works, he said "I've written it without ... enthusiasm."

In 1887, Tchaikovsky overcame his fear of performing and conducted his own works around the world. With renewed confidence, he began to write the Fifth Symphony.

But there was a further upheaval. In 1890, von Meck wrote that she could no longer support the composer financially. She never wrote to him again. Tchaikovsky did not need her money by now, but the end of the friendship devastated him. He felt "despair and a desire to flee ... to the world's end."

SADNESS AND GREATNESS

From this bitter period came one of Tchaikovsky's most sparkling works, *The Nutcracker* (1891). The same year, he conducted one of his works as the opening concert at Carnegie Hall in New York City. Then, in 1893, the composer's frustration found release in a work of intense passion and suffering, his Sixth Symphony, the *Pathétique*. As he planned it, he "frequently wept."

About a week after the symphony's premiere, Tchaikovsky died, on November 6, 1893. No one is sure why. There were rumors that he had died of cholera after drinking contaminated water.

MAJOR WORKS

1870	ROMEO AND JULIET
1875	SWAN LAKE
1878	EUGENE ONEGIN
1880	1812 OVERTURE
1888	SLEEPING BEAUTY
1891	THE NUTCRACKER
1893	SYMPHONY PATHÉTIQUE

GUSTAV MAHLER

Throughout his life, Mahler struggled against personal losses and anti-Jewish prejudice to achieve success as a conductor and composer. His symphonies, unpopular in his day, are now seen as the height of Romantic music.

Gustav Mahler was born into a Jewish family on July 7, 1860, in Austrian Bohemia, now part of the Czech Republic. At a young age, he showed great musical talent, and in 1875, his father sent him to the Austrian capital, Vienna, to begin his formal training.

When he graduated from the Vienna Conservatory in 1878, Mahler began work on his first pieces. But he soon discovered that the loneliness of composing did not suit him. So he decided to become a conductor as well.

EARLY CAREER

In the summer of 1880, Mahler made his conducting debut in Bad Hall, near Linz, Austria. For the next six years, he went from one conducting post to another. With each one came more success.

In 1886, Mahler moved to Leipzig, in eastern Germany, to become junior director of the opera house. It was a good position, but he did not keep it long. In 1888, he argued with the manager of the theater and resigned.

Within weeks, he had become director of the Royal Opera in Budapest, Hungary. It was a dazzling post for a 28-year-old, but Mahler soon proved himself. Although his ability as a conductor was in no doubt, his composing work attracted criticism. When he premiered his Symphony No. 1 in 1889, critics ridiculed it. This response, combined with the earlier deaths of his parents and his favorite sister, made this the unhappiest period of his life.

By spring 1891, Mahler's position at the Royal Opera in Budapest was under threat. His critics now blamed him for every mistake made by the opera company, whether or not it was his fault. His departure was a only matter of time.

Almost immediately, he became the conductor of the Hamburg Opera, a very prestigious post. During his six years in the German city, Mahler finally

Gustav Mahler
The exact date of this photograph is unknown, but it shows Mahler in the early 1890s, shortly after he moved to Hamburg.

88

became recognized as one of Europe's leading conductors. He was still relatively unknown as a composer, however: Not one ticket was sold for the premiere of his Symphony No. 2. He received another blow in 1895, when his brother, Otto, committed suicide. Mahler was so upset by this loss that he never spoke of it for the rest of his life.

Death and the meaning of life would be constant themes in Mahler's work. He wanted his symphonies to express the range of human emotions, from love and tenderness, through to loneliness, anguish, and self-doubt. Above all, his music conveyed a longing for something spiritual and eternal beyond the physical world.

Mahler used the orchestra in a new way. He employed vast numbers of musicians, with a wide variety of percussion instruments, to ensure the widest range of feelings. But Mahler's critics complained that his music sounded like "the roaring of lions and the screaming of terrified sheep."

RETURN TO VIENNA

In 1895, Mahler set his sights on becoming the director of the Imperial Vienna Opera, the greatest opera house in the world. In 1897, the post became available, and Mahler was appointed— but only after he had converted to Catholicism. As a Jew, he would never have gotten the job in a city where anti-Jewish prejudice was so rife.

Mahler's first season was a triumph. After this initial success, however, the critics turned against him. At first, Mahler was unconcerned, as audiences

MAHLER'S VIENNA

In 1900, Vienna was the capital of a huge, doomed empire. Its anxious citizens found a refuge in the arts.

During the 19th century, the once-mighty Austro-Hungarian empire slowly fell apart. All over its territory, nationalist groups, such as the Czechs and the Slavs, demanded independence from their Austrian masters in Vienna.

In its last years as an imperial capital, before the empire finally collapsed in World War I, the city witnessed an extraordinary burst of creativity. It provided the Viennese with a much-needed distraction from their worries. While artists such as Gustav Klimt and Egon Schiele were creating controversial, modern styles, Mahler was composing his epic symphonies. He had to wait until the

were still flocking to see his productions. But then he became the victim of a vicious smear campaign by anti-Jewish newspapers, which called him "that dwarf Jew." Events reached a climax in the winter of 1900, with the critics savaging everything Mahler produced. The tension made the composer sick, and he had to take a break in the country to restore his health.

end of his life to see success with these, but his productions of other composers' music drew large audiences to the prestigious Vienna Opera (*above*).

During his ten years in Vienna, Mahler controlled almost every aspect of the opera's administration. He chose the music, selected the musicians and singers, conducted most of the performances, and staged many of the productions himself. He even imposed his will on the audience. With one stern, forbidding glance, he could silence the noisiest of crowds.

When Mahler returned to Vienna in the fall of 1901, the situation was no better. The premiere of his Symphony No. 4 was a disaster, with critics calling it "musical madness."

This reaction made Mahler depressed and lonely. Then he met a society beauty called Alma Maria Schindler. They married in 1902. He was now happier than he had ever been before.

The birth of his first child, Maria Anna, gave him further pleasure. He now went out less and less, preferring to spend time with his new family.

SUCCESS AND SORROW

By this time, tastes were changing, and Mahler's music was being performed all over Europe. By 1907, these performances were taking up so much time that he had to resign his post at the Opera. At long last, he was a success as a composer. His joy came to an abrupt end, however, when Maria Anna suddenly died in the summer of 1907. Mahler was devastated. Soon after, his doctor told him he had a serious heart disease.

Mahler was determined to continue working as long as he could, and he now accepted an offer to conduct the Metropolitan Opera in New York. Before leaving Vienna, he conducted several farewell performances. Tearful audiences gave curtain call after curtain call to the equally emotional composer.

Mahler stayed in New York for three years. Soon after the 1911 season opened, his health worsened, and he returned to Vienna. Days later, on May 18, 1911, he died, at the age of just 50.

MAJOR WORKS

1878	THE SONG OF LAMENT
1901-02	SYMPHONY NO. 5
1906-07	SYMPHONY NO. 8
1907-09	THE SONG OF THE EARTH

GLOSSARY

academy A society formed to advance the practice of art, literature, or music.

apprentice A person who learns a trade or craft by working and studying with an experienced master.

canto A section, or subdivision, of a long narrative or epic poem.

classical The work of artists and writers who followed the styles and rules of ancient Greek and Roman art and literature.

classical music A term meaning the opposite of light, popular, or folk music. Classical music emphasizes order and clarity, and aims for formal beauty rather than emotional expression. It is considered to have permanent rather than short-lived value.

commission An order received by an artist, writer, or composer from a patron to produce a work of art, literature, or music.

complementary colors Each primary color—red, blue, and yellow—has a complementary color formed by a mixture of the other two.

composition The arrangement or organization of the various elements of a work of art, literature, or music.

concerto In the 17th century, the term could apply to any work combining voices and instruments; later it came to mean an instrumental work, usually in three movements.

engraving A method of making prints by cutting lines or dots into a hard surface, usually a metal plate.

Gothic novel Tales of the macabre, fantastic, and supernatural, usually set amid haunted castles, graveyards, and ruins. Such tales were fashionable in the 1790s and early 1800s.

landscape A kind of painting showing a view of natural scenery, such as mountains or forests.

mazurka A traditional Polish dance.

medium Term used to describe the various methods and materials of the artist, such as oil paint on canvas.

Neoclassicism The predominant artistic movement in Europe in the late 18th century and first years of the 19th century. It was characterized by a revival of the ideals of classical art, in an attempt to recapture the heroic spirit of ancient Greece and Rome.

ode A rhymed lyric poem, often in the form of an address, generally dignified in subject, feeling, and style.

oil paint A technique developed in the 15th century in which colors, or pigments, are mixed with the slow-drying and flexible medium of oil.

opera A dramatic musical work, first developed in late-16th-century Italy, in which the characters sing the text, accompanied by an orchestra.

patron A person or organization that asks an artist, writer, or composer to create a work of art, literature, or music.

portrait A drawing, painting, photograph, or sculpture that gives a likeness of a person and often provides an insight into his or her personality.

primary colors The three colors from which all others are derived—red, yellow, and blue.

print A picture produced by pressing a piece of paper against a variety of inked surfaces, including engraved metal plates and wooden blocks. There are several different methods of making prints, including engraving and etching.

quartet A musical piece usually for four string instruments or four singers.

Romanticism An early 19th-century European and American movement in art, literature, and music that was a reaction to the restraint and order of the 18th century. The Romantics emphasized the free expression of emotion and imagination, passion, love of nature and exotic places, liberty, and social reform. They rejected all strict rules governing the creation of art, and opposed technological progress.

Salon The official, and most important, state art exhibit of France, held in the Louvre Museum in Paris.

sketch A rough or quick version of a picture, often produced as a trial run for a more finished work.

still life A drawing or painting of objects that cannot move by themselves, such as fruit or flowers.

style The distinctive appearance of a particular artist, writer, or composer's work of art.

sublime An idea associated with expressing religious awe, vastness, natural magnificence, and strong emotion in art and literature, characteristic of the Romantic movement.

symbol An object which represents something else; for example, a dove commonly symbolizes peace.

symphony A serious orchestral work with several movements (often four) of different tempos, or speeds, and contrasting expressive qualities.

virtuoso A performer of exceptional skill, especially in the technical aspects of performance.

FURTHER READING

Anderson, Madelyn K. *Edgar Allan Poe: A Mystery.* Franklin Watts, 1993

Chapman, Laura. *Art: Images and Ideas,* "Discover Art" series. David Pubns., Inc., 1992

Copland, Aaron. *What to Listen for in Music.* NAL/Dutton, 1989

Hoffman, E.T. *Nutcracker.* HarcourtBrace, 1996

Janson, H.W. *The History of Art.* Abrams, 1995 (standard reference)

The New Grove Dictionary of Music and Musicians. Grove's Dictionaries of Music, 1980 (standard reference)

Powell, Jillian. *Art in the Nineteenth Century: Art and Artists.* Thomson Learning, 1994

Reyero, Carlos. *The Key to Art from Romanticism to Impressionism,* "Key to Art Books." Lerner Group, 1990

Shelley, Mary Wollstonecraft. *Frankenstein.* Adapted by Emily Hutchinson. American Guidance, 1995

Smith, Carter, ed. *Bridging the Continent: A Sourcebook on the American West.* Millbrook Press, 1992

Thompson, Wendy. *Ludwig Van Beethoven.* Viking Children's, 1991

Waldron, Ann. *Francisco Goya.* Abrams, 1992

INDEX

Entries in *italic* refer to books, paintings, photographs, or musical works. Page numbers in *italic* indicate illustrations. Page numbers in **bold** indicate main article.